"In a culture of achievement and personality, what a gift it is to be invited to unravel our story, drop our ego, and come home to our true selves. Elena's vulnerability and her skill as a teacher are awe-inspiring. Her prompts and practices are meaningful rituals—easy to weave into real life yet powerful enough to shift everything."

—GWYNETH PALTROW,
Academy Award–winning actor,
best-selling author, and founder of Goop

"Despite its title, this book holds many things: my attention, my admiration for its author, and even the softness and sweet sadness I feel when reading it. Don't miss this opportunity to discover your own rich emptiness by savoring *Hold Nothing* like a delicious, perfectly ripe fruit. Truly a treasure this weary world needs."

—JUDITH HANSON LASATER, PhD, PT, C-IAYT, E-RYT-500

"Elena Brower has once again offered us a radiant portal into inner realms. *Hold Nothing* is not just a book—it is a transmission of presence, a quiet summons from the soul. With the grace of a mystic and the skill of the true spiritual Renaissance woman that she is (painter, poet, teacher, meditator, healer, mother, friend), Elena weaves together teaching, story, inquiry, and vision—inviting us to enter the liminal spaces where the sacred speaks. This is a book to sit with, to pray with, to dream with. It is both a sanctuary and a compass, whispering us back to the center of what is most essential, most holy, and most alive within us."

—ELIZABETH GILBERT,
author of *Eat, Pray, Love* and *All the Way to the River*

"Elena is one of my heroes, and she has changed my life for the better. The wisdom and calm energy that Elena radiates is felt in these pages. *Hold Nothing* is the exact guidance all of us need as the world keeps changing. This is a must-read for anyone who wants to take their personal transformation work to a deeper level."

—YUNG PUEBLO,
New York Times best-selling author

"Elena Brower, who—try as you might—cannot be categorized to fit into any one descriptive box, has once again graced us with the preternatural gift that is her voice. *Hold Nothing*, a loving invitation for us to remember who we are without all the noise, is filled with all the signature honesty and wisdom we've come to know from Elena. 'Preternatural' can be defined as being suspended between the mundane and the miraculous, and not only is this book exactly that, but it's a reminder that we are too. This book is the North Star we desperately need right now."

—JENNIFER PASTILOFF,
best-selling author of *On Being Human*

"Having known Elena for two decades, she creates a field of attention and care through her work and relationships. *Hold Nothing* reflects her earnest path of empathy and inquiry, providing grounding and fortification whether you're in the midst of struggle or celebration."

—CHRISTY TURLINGTON BURNS,
founder and president of Every Mother Counts

"With life's most profound inquiries, I turn to sister and dearest friend Elena Brower for her listening and guidance. *Hold Nothing* drew me in, expanded my mind, and has me considering my work and life anew. Creating a true pause, this book is a gift, offering glimpses into her process but holding no answers, only the questions we need to be asking of ourselves."

—Dr. Gabrielle Lyon,
New York Times best-selling author of *Forever Strong*

"This is a personal and beautiful invitation to become intimate through mindfulness of body, heart, and mind. A guide to true belonging, asking us to face our deepest yearning and our greatest fears. No part left out."

—Frank Ostaseski,
author of *The Five Invitations*

"*Hold Nothing* is a gift from Elena Brower. Her ability to share profound teachings in a simple and exquisite way makes her one of our most prolific storytellers. This book reminds us of how attentive we can be to the details of this life."

—Carrie-Anne Moss, mother, actor,
and founder of Annapurna Living

"Have you ever gotten very quiet and closed your eyes halfway, such that objects lose their edges and the world becomes mere shadow and light? Just playful shimmers. And then slowly turned that same quality of attention around toward yourself? What's there? I feel the same way inside of *Hold Nothing*. Light, unadorned, liminal. Neither here nor there. Elena bottles her own essence, perfuming us into stillness and peace."

—JEFF KRASNO, author of *Good Stress*
and cofounder and CEO of Commune

"In her insightful book, my dear sister Elena Brower shares her journey, her process, and her profound reverence, gently yet irresistibly encouraging us to release and create space for what truly matters. True to Elena's style, her words and stories (which I adore!) are as poetic, inspiring, meaningful, and beautiful as a Zen garden. *Hold Nothing* serves as a reminder to approach and embrace our own lives with the same care, artistry, and love."

—DEVA PREMAL,
Grammy-nominated mantra singer

"*Hold Nothing* is more than a book—it's an offering, a blessing, a quiet revolution. Elena Brower, who is so dear to me, has a rare and radiant gift: she transmits ancient spiritual wisdom with a clarity and grace that lands straight in the heart. In these pages, she weaves timeless truth with modern resonance, crafting something both grounding and elevating. It's a soul companion, a steadying breath, a sacred conversation. There is no better gift for this moment—and no one I trust more to offer it."

—LAURA McKOWEN, best-selling author of
We Are the Luckiest and *Push Off from Here*

"Elena has a way of creating nurturing, contemplative spaces in which we enter and instantly feel safe, seen, and at home. *Hold Nothing* is a love letter about how we experience the world, full of questions and vulnerability, care and consistency. Open this book and come to know yourself better through Elena's vision and heart."

—SARA SZAL GOTTFRIED, MD,
New York Times best-selling author of
The Hormone Cure

"*Hold Nothing* is a luminous act of devotion to the human spirit. With rare artistry, grace, and quiet courage, Elena Brower offers a tender remembrance—a map not toward more doing but toward a necessary unbecoming. This book is a gift for all who long to return to the sacred simplicity of being who they truly are."

—MEGAN DALLA-CAMINA, author of
Women Rising and *Simple Soulful Sacred*

"With *Hold Nothing*, Elena Brower offers us a contemplative refuge—a space where presence, release, and remembrance meet. Through her words and luminous artwork, she invites us into an intimate dialogue with the soft, transformative power of letting go. This book isn't just read—it's felt. An essential guide for new and experienced meditators to cultivate lasting resilience."

—SIERRA CAMPBELL,
founder of Choose Nurture

"Elena Brower is a national, no—scratch that—*global* treasure. It is a rare and miraculous thing when such deep wisdom, artistic vision, compassion, elegance, generosity, and grace meet up in the same capacious heart. I keep her words near me at all times, and I am better for it."

—DANI SHAPIRO, best-selling author
and host of *Family Secrets* podcast

"*Hold Nothing* is a masterwork of soft power. Through its pages, Elena becomes our brilliant witness and guide, leading us through the sacred act of surrender. Not surrender as loss. But as *liberation*. Each page is a lantern for the darkened places within us, illuminating the subtle beauty that presence, pause, and release can offer. Her invitations, reflections, and insights are medicine for the soul, quietly waiting for us when our spirits need them most."

—CORY ALLEN, author of
Brave New You and *Now Is the Way*

"What happens when we appreciate the timeline of our own becoming, when we look at the poetic details that create our life story, and then let it all go? In *Hold Nothing*, Elena Brower reminds us that, with practice, we are able to shed and change, to renew and grow. Each chapter offers us permission to build new pathways; each word is an arrow of illumination bringing us closer to the healing art of openness and release."

—JACQUELINE SUSKIN, poet, educator,
and author of *The Verse for Now*

"Deeply spacious, reverent, and intimate, *Hold Nothing* is a soft landing for the soul and a steadying compass for this disorienting time. The structure is elegant and clear, while the writing is spacious enough to let the reader really feel themselves within the pauses."

—TRACEE STANLEY, author of
Radiant Rest and *The Luminous Self*

"*Hold Nothing* is a soft and steady companion for the soul. With honesty and grace, Elena Brower reminds us that healing isn't about becoming someone new—it's about returning home to ourselves, again and again. This book is both mirror and medicine: it invites us to release what no longer serves, to soften into the truth of who we are, and to root ourselves in what's real. A generous offering for anyone learning to let go with love."

—ALEX ELLE,
author of *How We Heal*

"Elena Brower, a dear sister and friend, does it again—among many gifts that pour through the meticulously honed instrument that is her life, she reminds us that not only do words matter but that by attending to their sacred qualities, we create new pathways for ourselves, one another, and our world to come home. My heart throbs each time I enter into the stream of Elena's writing voice. May this latest graceful offering, *Hold Nothing*, remind us of the sacred and that everyone and everything deserves the revealing gaze we give to the sacred. May 'grandmother's heart' more deeply awaken in each and every one of us as we use this book as a mirror to what wants to grow in each of our lives and the many small moments."

—SCOTT SCHWENK, teacher and creator of
The Choice to Grow podcast

"More than a book, *Hold Nothing* is a luminous braid of personal story, grounded guidance, and evocative contemplations. Elena's words blossom from the depths of silence. With generosity and warmth, she guides us in cultivating an inner garden we can harvest to nourish our true self and feed the hungry world."

—MIRABAI STARR, author of
Wild Mercy and *Ordinary Mysticism*

"Sharing a friendship with Elena since our twenties has meant walking alongside her through seasons of growth, change, and deep devotion to becoming a more complete human. *Hold Nothing* is the embodiment of that path—an offering steeped in hard-won wisdom, humility, and presence. In a time when so many of us feel disconnected from ourselves, each other, and the living world, this book is a luminous, tenderly pressing invitation to return to what matters most: our aliveness, our inner knowing, and our attunement to the natural rhythm of life. I'll be gifting this book often."

—AMY IPPOLITI, author of
The Art and Business of Teaching Yoga

"*Hold Nothing* is for you if you're tired of holding everything. On these pages, Elena Brower whispers her graceful invitation to a life lived lightly. Full of poise, gentleness, and effortless clarity, reading this book is like sitting down with Elena at her tea table, receiving her personal experiences and insights."

—GEERTJE COUWENBERGH,
author and creator of *365 Days of Writing*

"Throughout her career, Elena Brower has consistently and generously opened the door to her innermost sanctum, offering us a mirror, an invitation to map ourselves more truly. *Hold Nothing* is the fruit of her deep apprenticeship to silence, her steady navigation of the inner landscape through the lens of Zen. This is a book of intimacy—with ourselves, with life, with the practices that call us home. Here, Elena weaves esoteric wisdom with the groundedness of lived experience so that we too might, as she writes, 'join with [our] own life in a new way.' Through her vulnerability, her story, her offering, she lets us glimpse the parts of ourselves that, when seen, can set us free. As a longtime friend, student, and witness to Elena's work, I've watched in awe as she lives these teachings with complete devotion and grace. This book is, at times, a reflection of her journey and, at others, an invocation to a deeper version of our own."

—ALLY BOGARD,
teacher and author of *The Quiet Teachers*

"Everyone has glimpsed this deeply held longing: we desperately want to be better friends to ourselves. As a consequence of our most vulnerable longing, the vice grip we put on shame, and the 'protective' silence around it all, we search for external signs from those who truly know how to befriend themselves. Let that search end now. In *Hold Nothing*, Elena Brower shares her challenges and aspirations in a way that gently leads you back into yourself to find the friend you've always had."

—PAMELA AYO YETUNDE, ThD,
author of *Dearly Beloved: Prince, Spirituality,*
and *This Thing Called Life*

"Having personally witnessed the extraordinary bloom of Elena Brower's efforts in the world and the way she has positively impacted countless lives, it makes perfect sense that *Hold Nothing* shows up now to serve the considerable needs of the hour. This book is an invitation to walk the never-ending Path of Discovery . . . in a state of utter surrender."

—TOMMY ROSEN,
best-selling author and founder of Recovery 2.0

"With the kind of clarity that only comes from having walked through fire and come out the other side with grace intact, Elena Brower invites us into the radical act of returning to the place many of us fear going: back to ourselves. Through story, reflection, and exquisite stillness, *Hold Nothing* offers a blueprint for coming home—to presence, to purpose, to the parts of ourselves we've been too afraid to meet. Elena is one of the voices I turn to when I am lost, and this book is filled with her wisdom, which I trust so dearly."

—AMANDA DE CADENET,
host, photographer, and advocate

"Elena Brower's words will nourish you in the deepest of ways. It takes courage to step back from the noise and step back into your true expression. *Hold Nothing* is not just a book—it's your map and your companion for the practice of coming home to yourself, again and again."

—KEMI NEKVAPIL, author of
The Gift of Asking and *Power*

"In reading *Hold Nothing*, I felt myself return to the pulse of life with more profound reverence. Each page breathes. This book is more than something you read—it's something you feel. A quiet current drawing you closer to your sacred interior. Elena's voice is both anchor and invitation, guiding us through the rawness of becoming with grace, humility, and artistry. Her work is a sacred tether to the living moment, to the beauty that lives and aches in everything."

—SARAH BLONDIN,
author of *Heart Minded*

ELENA BROWER

Hold Nothing

AN INVITATION TO LET GO
AND COME HOME TO YOURSELF

SHAMBHALA

Shambhala Publications, Inc.
2129 13th Street
Boulder, Colorado 80302
www.shambhala.com

Cover art: Elena Brower
Cover design: Daniel Urban-Brown
Interior design: Toni Tajima

9 8 7 6 5 4 3 2 1

First Edition
Printed in the United States of America

Shambhala Publications makes every effort to print on acid-free, recycled paper.
Shambhala Publications is distributed worldwide by Penguin Random House, Inc.,
and its subsidiaries.

LIBRARY OF CONGRESS CATALOGING-IN-PUBLICATION DATA
Names: Brower, Elena author
Title: Hold nothing: an invitation to let go and come home to yourself / Elena Brower.
Description: First edition. | Boulder, Colorado: Shambhala, [2025] |
   Includes bibliographical references. |
Identifiers: LCCN 2024054269 | ISBN 9781645473022 trade paperback
Subjects: LCSH: Self-realization | Self-perception | Meditation | Spiritual life
Classification: LCC BF637.S4 B81165 2025 | DDC 158.1—dc23/eng/20250410
LC record available at https://lccn.loc.gov/2024054269

The authorized representative in the EU for product safety and
compliance is eucomply OÜ, Pärnu mnt 139b-14, 11317 Tallinn, Estonia,
hello@eucompliancepartner.com.

To the teachers who've graced my path, in every form.

CONTENTS

ACKNOWLEDGMENTS

Thank you to James Benard and Kevin Sullivan of Benard Creative for your diligent care with the art in this book.

Thank you to Sara Bercholz for your trust, friendship, and steady presence over so many seasons.

Thank you to Beth Frankl for your eyes, ears, heart, and mind on the editing of this book; your insights shaped it in ways seen and unseen.

Thank you to Deva Shantay for seeing this chapter of my life first and giving it a name.

Thank you to each human mentioned in these pages— family, dear friends, and respected teachers—for your integral role in my formation and for walking alongside me in ways both direct and subtle.

Thank you to the generous friends, clients, and colleagues who've offered your words in support of this work; your reflections are a gift I'll never forget.

Finally, thank you to you, dear reader; may this book meet you precisely where you are.

INTRODUCTION

Opening a book can be an entrance to new lands within yourself—views and vantage points you may have not yet encountered. In finding our way together in these pages, two simple words will guide us: *practice* and *respect*.

Practice is fundamental to our conscious evolution; we're always practicing—how to be with ourselves, how to be with each other. Welcoming the settling and quieting of your inner life requires practice, as does treating yourself and others with kindness.

Alongside practice, or perhaps embedded deeply within it, is respect—a quality we learn we can bring to each moment, a sense of heart-based urgency to offer our attention and care to craft interactions laden with the deep listening our world needs.

As we enter into this exploration, I humbly bring a burgeoning reverence for Zen as it has threaded through my heart over these recent years, informing how I walk, sit, move, care, and listen. The practice is fully present and alive within me.

If you're willing, as you read on, bring yourself into an artful, caring dialogue with your own heart as your most trustworthy guide here.

Once in a long while, you receive an intriguing invitation to join with your own life in a new way. To see details with fresh eyes, to evolve the way you're walking into your days, your relationships, your creativity, your own care.

Such invitations are fleeting: slanting sun casting the shadow of an elder tree on your path. Words of an attentive teacher piercing your heart. Silence of the morning before minds begin thinking.

When that invitation arrives, the questions to ask are the most simple and direct: What is being asked of me? How can I come to know myself more intimately? And with that knowledge, what can I do to serve my community, our humanity?

This book is an invitation to come alongside yourself, to experience new ways to approach your own heart, to listen well, and to love yourself with rigor, certainty, warmth, and tenderness. To live deeply and reverently in the smallest details. Zen practice has been a profound teacher to me in embracing all of this. It's taught me that when we let go of who we *thought* we had to be, we can stop reaching and truly connect with the reality of our surroundings to create the intimacy we crave. I hope that the experiences of this that I share with you in these pages will help spur your own journey.

I'm writing this to you from a traditional tatami room in the countryside just outside Kyoto, Japan. After a short sitting meditation at my host's altar, I'm steeped in details. A small white porcelain vase with one white tulip and three long stalks of grass is perched on a lacquered black tray.

Indigo *shibori* textiles adorn this table at which I'm sitting, cross-legged on a thin pillow, wooden sliding doors demarcating the small bedrooms surrounding my writing space. Thoughtful piles of tiny teacups sit patiently on a center tray. Outside the window, impossibly neat rows of *Camellia sinensis* growing on rolling hills, my hands dancing across my keyboard to capture this magnificent silence. Dashi warming on the stove, the scent of dinner's impending nourishment.

Are you sensing the invitation to notice where you are right now, *wherever* you are right now? Can you practice being with yourself in a more reverent, observant way? And can you touch into the respect at the root of this moment?

The writings and prompts in these pages ask only for your artful attention and compassionate care of yourself. We're entering into what you may find is your independence, full self-acceptance, utter simplicity, and possibly a deepening compassion for yourself and all beings.

The prompts will ask you to tune in to your surroundings, forget yourself to know yourself, and perhaps more crucially, fully accept yourself. Such support for oneself is a building block of maturity. This is how you will discover what's being asked of you.

Please be attentive to the rhythm in these pages; if you are willing to slow down, stop completely at times, and take a breath, the inquiries can come alive in you.

○

Before we embark on this journey together, please allow me a moment of your generous attention to bring you back to where this all began for me. My own journey of self in snapshots.

- For my seventh birthday, my parents gift me a drafting table, a professional chair, a caddy for my art supplies, and a seriousness about my art-making that changes my life. My mom introduces me to artists and artwork, helping me open my eyes to see differently. When I look back now, it's as though she was doing for me what she wished someone would've done for her: inviting me to be an artist. The moment of sitting down at that table for the first time is precisely when I begin believing in myself.

- At eleven years old, I'm sitting in Central Synagogue in Rockville Centre, New York, next to my mother, tears running down her face as she chants the Shema. The part about inscribing "these words on the doorposts of your house, and on your gates" seems to send her deeply into her heart. Now when I hear those words, I feel an instant connection to history, lineage, family, and direction, but also with a sense of buoyancy. Those words always come to me along with a deluge of cleansing tears that connect my mother and me.

- Thirty years old, just months from beginning my teaching journey in earnest, drifting off on a yoga mat at the end of a demanding, carefully sequenced class, body deeply at rest for the first time in years, I realize I *have* a body, worthy of care, precision, gentleness. And I begin wondering if I might someday be able to offer someone else this sensation of nurturance.

- Forty years old, tucked between two dear women friends in a training I hope will never end, learning how to teach yoga with care, warmth, and clarity and feeling as though I've been led here. Experiencing well-crafted classes, meticulous alignment, live *kirtan*, and some of the most challenging assignments of my life, I feel at home professionally, a feeling that will create a lasting imprint on my psyche, a barometer for every job I'll endeavor to do in the future.

- Fifty-two years old, seated in the zendo during a monthlong practice period at the Upaya Zen Center, tears falling into my hands, palms pressed together in *gassho* at the end of a dharma talk that awakens something ancient within me, a subtler resonance I've not previously known.

Each of these experiences wells up in the book you hold in your hands.

And now as I did then, I find potency and inspiration in the silences of Nature, in the green trees, the piñons, the desert flowers and smallest stones, in handcrafted ceramics, handwoven textiles, and handmade books. The invitations to get quiet and see, to trust and serve, to feel and become lead me swiftly back to myself.

Studying Srividya and Tantric philosophy early on in my formation helped me consider becoming the elder I've always sought, an unfolding process. Learning to steward myself emotionally in times of conflict through the wisdom in the Yoga Sutras of Patanjali, the Upanisads, and, more recently, Zen koans has helped me release the sense of a permanent identity and stay open to my own inevitable evolution. Everything is always in flux. Practicing and facilitating yoga asanas in several traditions from *vinyasa* to Katonah gives me a ground of being, yielding a combination of physical strength and softness amidst the chaos of a constantly shifting landscape, an appreciation for the art of breathing, and an understanding of internal hydraulics.

Encountering the Upaya Zen Center's comprehensive virtual offerings in early 2020 was a grounding gift to me, one that is continually unfolding. Zen practice recalibrates my energy and returns my attention to an ever-expanding intimacy with myself as I am. This not-knowing, dropping the persona I've spent so long building, allows me to simply *be* in this new strata of engagement to benefit my community, working with hospice patients, incarcerated men, and grieving families.

Zazen, or sitting meditation, is a practice of sitting still, noticing the phenomena of thoughts, emotions, stories, and fears arising and receding in my awareness, then realizing I am not these thoughts my brain is secreting, nor am I these emotions my body seems to be circulating. Something bigger and more generous is happening here. I'm learning to trust in this practice of sitting, also known as *shikantaza*—trusting in the practice itself, trusting in these wild rides in the mind, trusting in my willingness to know nothing whatsoever, and trusting in my capacity to stop adding to the suffering and instead endure and adapt, with resiliency and kindness.

At first, the unfathomable stillness of meditation threatened everything I thought I had to uphold; mostly the shiny façade of being busy, feeling important. Slowly, the dissolution of specialness began to reveal a needed perspective on our sameness, our interconnectedness, the soul-level similarities amidst our perceived differences.

Meditation brings stability to both mind and heart, refining my communication inwardly and outwardly, growing my capacity for empathy. Importantly, sitting brings me closer to the unalterable impermanence holding us all. We are here to be in relationship, to grow old, to die. Sitting, to me, slows down time, some days exasperatingly so, but it's ameliorating my tendency to cling to thoughts of something better, something missing. Sitting moves me toward appreciation, to living my full life each day with more care and contentment.

The practice of zazen has since become a calibrating balm to my movement practices. Around the time of this writing, I received the Zen precepts, thereby entering the stream of teachings in the lineage of Soto Zen. I've taken vows to do no harm, to benefit all beings, to seek nothing, to steep myself in the practice, and to allow the practice to work on me. Just a handful of days before writing this, I had the occasion to visit Eiheiji, the temple where this lineage was brought into being by ancestor Eihei Dogen more than eight hundred years ago.

A source of scholarship, maturity, compassion, and dignity, Dogen's words and the practice he encouraged give rise to a certain acceptance of all that is. Just this, precisely as it is. Instead of resisting, I'm learning how to flow and move with reality, to find joy and ease in grave difficulty, gradually dropping who I *thought* I needed to be: one who was achieving and striving. I'm turning my attention toward humble studentship instead of grabbing and grasping at what I think I need, using the ingredients of my life to engage with my community, serve others in their awakening, and maybe experience some moments of awakening within myself.

Discerning how to be a *human* is what I'm learning in this field of practice. It may take many lifetimes, but I'm seeing how dropping the previous persona is clearing space and building more capacity for being of benefit in this world.

So what's being asked of me?

- That I share this slow, steadying process of letting go of certain aspects of myself I've spent much of my adult life trying to cultivate. That I continue to go back to the beginning.

- That I keep dropping the layers of personality and habit patterns that have served purposes at various stages. Even though they've helped me develop tenacity, confidence, even studentship and diligence, those patterns are standing in the way of simpler priorities like respect and intimacy, outwardly and inwardly.

- That I amplify experiences of reverence that have punctuated and propelled my life and art from childhood to this day.

In these pages I ask you to take my hand, slow down, and listen well, to know yourself deeply and to tend to your steadiness as a practice. Such acceptance and intimacy reveal new closeness in relationship with others, more robust connectivity with those in your community, and greater capacity to learn what's being asked of you so you can serve the healing of our world. We'll move with care to continue learning together.

As an evolution of, and departure from, my journals *Practice You* and *Being You*, *Hold Nothing* is a comprehensive, contemplative guidebook in which I offer you insights, teachings, and experiences that have simplified my understanding of this great matter of life. The urgent practice of simply showing up, being present for our lives precisely as we are, and recalling our intention for being in this field of practice is where we'll linger.

Whether you're entering this experience with a lifetime of spiritual study or none at all, approach these pages with the mind of a beginner and a heart of service, knowing you're warmly welcomed into these inquiries no matter where you begin. Simple meditation instructions that you may decide to use are located in the backmatter for you.

Through prompts and pockets of emptiness throughout this book, you're invited to chronicle your questions, to dive into your present feelings and boundaries. You're invited to recognize and cultivate a burgeoning sense of trust in yourself and to remember you're not here to solve anything; this is a practice of becoming more present to the questions.

Blanketed in silence and deliberate subtlety, these pages are portals through which you can welcome moments of acknowledgment and flow within yourself. Each prompt is a chance to discover what's alive for you, what's being asked of you right now, intending to welcome you back to an emergent understanding within yourself.

Introspection takes dedication. Taking the time to discover yourself and find out where you can serve is a choice that benefits all. May you journey through these pages toward a sense of grounded, supportive presence within yourself, so you can begin the lifelong process of steadying yourself to offer that stability to our tangled world. May these pages remind you to practice with reverence for the lessons that land in your life.

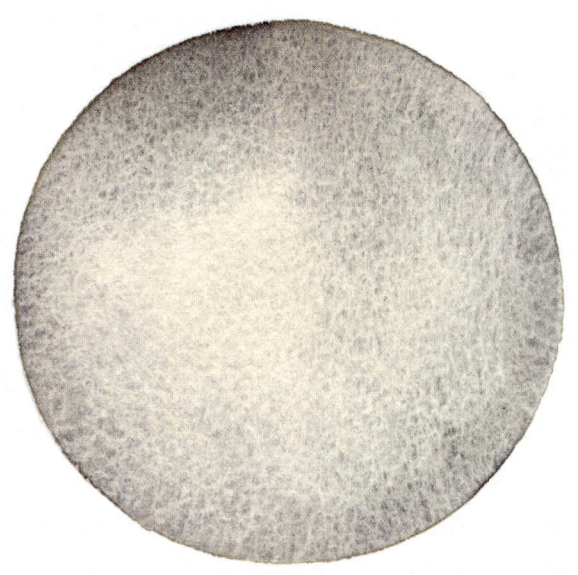

1
Opening into
Your True Self

With implications of making yourself available and settling into infinite uncertainty, *opening* is where we begin
our journey together. Opening into presence, into compassion, into listening, into love, into tenderness, into
impermanence . . .

A sense of release is what happens when you finally
let go of what you know, how you look, what you do, who
you thought you needed to be to access yourself. When
you savor *being* yourself, releasing what you thought you
needed to know and being present with your experiences
of grief and beauty, day after day, until you become a deepening well of emotional understanding and intelligence.

Opening. Releasing.

OPEN INTO PRESENCE

Opening to what's true now takes courage, a touch of enthusiasm, and abiding patience. Begin with the willingness to open yourself inwardly, so you can release what you *think* is true to be present to what's *actually* happening.

Morning five of a monthlong Zen meditation practice period; my mind is *just* beginning to quiet down. Thirty- or sixty-minute sittings are interspersed with walking meditation, periods of tending to our shared spaces, nourishing meals, and times for study. Forty of us are slowly beginning to drop into the schedule here for one month, which feels simultaneously calming and daunting.

Standing in the meditation hall with hands folded in prayer, plenty of missteps in bowing, sitting, kneeling, chanting, and walking. My inexperience must be glaringly obvious. Will I ever learn how to properly honor these practices? Will I ever open into this version of myself I dream of becoming?

Realizing so many ingrained layers of my personality needing to be released, I find myself weeping unexpectedly for the better part of days two and three. Each ceremony, chant, and bow feels like I'm bidding a previous version of myself farewell, making intimate contact with a new understanding that feels distant but distinctly my own. Seeing how hard I can be on myself, decades of judgment and misunderstanding rise to the surface of my mind and create litanies of thought to keep me busy as I sit. I have no idea if I'm doing this correctly.

In a practice interview with one of the teachers, I'm reminded of how each moment gives way to another breath and everything is always changing. I realize I'll never be finished with this process of unfolding, then I release that realization too.

Roshi Joan Halifax, abbot of Upaya, offers us a few words for our personal practice day, gently and precisely reminding us that we're here to steady ourselves in order to be of some benefit as we move through our fraught, fraying world.

She offers us the gift of noble silence for the remainder of the day, establishing a quality of presence to meet the churn of our time. I'm wondering if I can meet myself in the silence. Before I can appreciate how sobering and stabilizing silence can be, I spend the first day struggling with it, concerned with what others must think of me, how I look, and who's watching. Am I doing any of this correctly? Can anyone see that I'm not who I've been, who I said I'd become?

The whole surface is unraveling, and I have no idea who I am in this quiet. But I know what I must do, so I keep opening, releasing. Opening. Releasing. Letting go of layers of personality, programming, and ways of coping and relating. There is fear here and also a sense of community in the silence. A knowing that this is just the beginning.

The topography of persona comes alive for me in that silence, where I begin to clearly perceive the protective layers of my personality accrued over time. Diligence protects me from conflict, judgment. I can see where I try to meet others' gazes, to connect, to affirm myself. Vigilance regarding others' struggles keeps me out of trouble, out of their way—just like when I was younger with my parents. Being a "good girl" smooths everything over, making it all okay. Being "good" means everyone will love me and care about me.

Those layers—born of early-life necessity—carried me into adulthood and now come into question every time I walk, sit, clean, and chop, precisely because I cannot distract myself with upholding them. Uncomfortably, a closeness with myself begins to emerge, then an intimacy with the community around me, even without words. Everything comes into stark relief. The topography of a fearful, fake personality asking to be shed.

Who am I really?

Are these layers of personality just expressions of my own fears of failure and insufficiency? Seeing how much I've cared about people seeing me, liking me, and learning that I can shed those layers of fear and insufficiency, I'm coming into a new appreciation for who I am beneath all of that. And I'm realizing that allowing those fears to dissolve is a sort of offering I make to the field of practice, to the overall energy of my house and my family.

What layers of personality might you be able to shed?

What aspects of your daily life are impacted by fears or feelings of insufficiency?

Who are you beneath those feelings?

Beneath those layers, can you appreciate the heart of who you are?

OPEN INTO COMPASSION

Our task is to see our traces of pain as our map to compassion; tracking struggle as a signpost pointing toward a fresh perspective on the whole matter of your existence. Opening to compassion is a moment-to-moment endeavor of letting go of discursive thought and acknowledging, *Now I feel lost—can I summon compassion for myself? What does compassion look like this time? Can I drop the concept of "lost" or "found" and just breathe to open until this new tension in my body passes?*

Suffering is always inviting you to a sense of compassion for all that is. It might be that simple, but practice is everything.

I'm forty-four years young when I first learn about the concept of compassion in earnest. I'm a few days sober, weeping in my bath, not sure I'll make it through the hour without numbing the ache I'm feeling with *something*. Anything. I'm trying to put on a brave face, three days clean. Right now I'm suffering. I close my eyes, remembering a question a trusted friend asked me recently: "How can you serve when you're numbing yourself?"

Feeling the next breath rush into my body, I realize this is all I need—one full breath—to dissolve my fear and soften this sensation of suffering. Then I realize the sensation of suffering isn't actually *suffering*—it's a *story* I'm telling. It's a story about how helpful being high can be, which is no longer true for me. Compassion comes over me in a wave. I feel a few cells inside my lungs plumping up; one breath can change everything.

The first phone calls to dear women friends in the early days of sobriety serve to recalibrate my being. To my surprise, they affirm my choice, quietly, making this transition more plausible for me: "Yes, I'll walk into this with you. No, you won't lose my friendship; we can stay close as you navigate this. Yes, I'll still come over for afternoons in the sunshine even though we won't be smoking. And no, I don't feel pressured by your choice—I'm rethinking how I treat myself as a result." And some friends fell away, not on the same page.

Since that day in 2014, when one breath changed everything, I've been engaging in study, therapy, and meditation, practicing and embodying care and consistent compassion for myself, even alongside these traces of painful grasping in my tissues, reminding me to stay the course. Opening into compassion for myself in that clarifying, tender time led to a deepening of a few friendships in my life, nourishing me deeply during this past decade and reminding me of who I am as a mother, a daughter, a sister, a friend. Instead of contracting the aperture of our friendship as I chose to clear my mind and release my addictions, each friend who stayed in their own way opened to my vulnerability, held my hand, asked good questions.

Can you consider your pain an invitation to a new way of seeing things, to dropping the narrative and becoming more intimate with reality *as it is*? In the tub that day, the one breath I took in became the antidote to another day of addiction.

By learning and cultivating more skillful ways of relating to ourselves and each other, we practice bringing more kindness to our thinking, even when pain is present. This is the intimacy of the practice of zazen; befriending and caring for our difficulties while sitting, we become more intimate with despair, judgment, entanglements, and confusion. We can witness these experiences and become more skillful with our own pain. Compassion isn't about ridding ourselves of suffering; it's about relating to our heartbreak and discomfort with care and respect.

Have you ever embarked upon a journey in a new direction, personally or professionally, longing for the support of those closest to you?

Who showed up for you in those seasons? What good questions did they offer you?

Might you find a way to thank the supportive human(s) here?

Can you practice relating to your *own* discomfort or heartbreak with more care and respect, as though relating to a dear friend?

OPEN INTO LISTENING

Creating a field of generous attention and care takes practice. As we make our initial attempts at listening with precision and gentleness, we are changed slowly and quietly from within. You might notice you're walking in the world with fewer words and more creativity as you grow older. You might experience a level of kindness toward yourself that feels like a release of linear thinking into a more spacious sense of inner freedom, which is precisely the offering you'll make to those in your life with whom you've not been listening attentively.

It's the height of the pandemic, our family of three is cooking together most nights, sitting for dinners together, learning about and relating to each other for the first time. Remember that moment on Earth when we were shopping in nearly empty markets, driving on nearly empty roads, and feverishly cleaning our groceries?

During this intimate time together, we're doing our best to make sense of it all. We laugh often, respecting and relating carefully to each other.

We learn how to really, actually *listen*, mostly succeeding at this subtle, vital practice.

Attending school in New York City virtually for the final months of that year, my son needs to be heard and supported in new ways. He and I realize how important it is to take care of each other, which doesn't come easily. Over the course of several heated discussions, some of which involve me shouting recklessly, expressing old patterns that no longer belong to me, I make a practice of hearing his requests for more autonomy, trusting in his capacity to organize his days. He begins choosing his own bedtime, setting his own alarm to wake up; I don't intervene. He begins to feel trustworthy. As he learns to trust *himself*, he learns he can also trust me.

Instead of blocking out his perspective, listening helps me cultivate a deepening, calming respect for myself and for him. In the years since, this choice to listen well to him has borne out; we've both deconstructed ancestral assumptions about how parents and kids *should* interact, creating a new language of our own, hilariously and respectfully calling one another "boss"—and making allowances leading to moments in which all we can do amidst the logistics is laugh.

I don't expect him to be "the child"—I simply expect respect, the same respect I offer to him. In releasing the hierarchical thinking, we keep finding one another on a level playing field. Boundaries and certain household rules still apply, of course, but we've established a solid mutual trust.

We did it. We both grew up.

No matter with whom we're in contact—partner, parent, sibling, child, friend—our shared invitation is to open to listening with respect. It takes practice to hear those closest to us when we've established or accepted certain fixed ideas about how we're meant to relate.

Particularly when you differ in opinion or belief, to whom can you listen more respectfully without needing to agree?

Were you or were you not respected by your caretaker(s) as a child, and what was the impact of that imprint on your adult understanding of respect?

Did you experience any teacher or mentor offering you respect that surprised you?

To whom can you offer more respect or listening in your close vicinity? A child, a parent, a sibling, a friend? Can you track your efforts and return to this page to remind yourself of the impression your respect has made?

OPEN INTO LOVE

To learn how to open ourselves when we want to close, to let go, to notice how much we ruminate when things hurt and to surrender that too. To practice releasing our assumptions, dying all the time to what we *thought* defined our reality.

> *And if we do, we might also start to perceive*
> *the interdependence of suffering and joy—*
> *that life and death are not separate but intertwined*
> *like roots deep in the earth.*
> —JOAN HALIFAX, *Being with Dying*

Sitting on my nine-year-old son Jonah's bed in New York, playing air hockey, procrastinating on cooking dinner and preparing for a class I'm meant to teach in Brooklyn tonight, my phone rings; it's my sister. My mother's had a heart attack, and it's likely going to mean the end of her life. Right now, today, or tomorrow.

Moving about carefully so I don't start uncontrollably weeping, I'm packing luggage, offering a few measured tips to Jonah about what to pack. I can hear my mother's voice as a whisper in my head: "Nice shoes. Bring some nice shoes to go with the dress."

She's referencing the funeral dress I'd just placed in the garment bag, matter-of-factly.

Next stop, Penn Station, where I'll board the train to the town where she gave birth to me, to the same hospital where she will take her last breaths in about forty hours from now.

I spent so much of my twenties and thirties wishing she'd give me a little more space, and every time I close my eyes during the next two days, *those* moments are all I can see in the slideshow of my consciousness. Her longing face pleading with me, *Why not just stay?* Forgiving myself will become a practice in the coming days, weeks, years.

Every time I close my eyes and open myself to feel, I keep seeing her biggest, most engaging smiles from my childhood, when she was *everything*. My practice is to keep opening to that love, no matter what I'm doing.

After she passes, painful states acutely arise then pass. In so many times since, I've watched it happen, both in zazen and in my day-to-day.

Learning to clearly observe the changing nature of the mind, at once sullen, longing to just call her, talk to her, tears falling, then the next moment, I hear her offering some sage wisdom that stops me from falling into an unhelpful thought pattern. She's right here. She's always here.

The interdependence and simultaneity of suffering and joy is incontrovertible evidence of impermanence. Each time we let go of some old pattern or belief, a part of us passes on, revealing more depth and presence. Our work is to engage the energy beneath the passing emotions, to soothe ourselves with unshakable presence. We're here to remember that love never dissipates, it endures with tenacity, within every deep sorrow.

Call upon a season of grief in your life. Turn it over, open it up, and look at and into it.

Can you feel yourself opening into the unshakable, immutable love that endures through the process and experience of grief?

Is there anyone with whom you wish you'd have spent more time now that they're gone? If you'd find it healing, write them a note about what you would do together if you had another few hours with them.

In what realm of your current experience are you finding suffering and joy existing simultaneously?

What pattern or belief might be best released in this season of your life?

OPEN INTO TENDERNESS

The tenderness with which you address what's present within yourself, especially when it hurts, allows the pain to pass through the field of your awareness with less attachment to an outcome or even a desire for more ease. No matter what's present, tenderness as a practice is a gift we give to ourselves and everyone in our sphere.

It's been eight years since my mom's passing, and grief still lingers on certain days. Learning to hold waves of intense sadness carefully, like I'd hold a child, a practice of tenderness has begun to suffuse my approach to other matters in my life, making available more care and openness.

When I allow the softening, I continue to sense more caring in my heart as time passes.

Today, as my son is pulling his car out of the driveway heading to his job at a local restaurant, I find myself standing in the garage again to say goodbye, as is our routine. A sense of distant, tidal sadness stealthily washes over me, a tall wave. I stand very still, returning myself to the present, back from the future, acknowledging my grief tenderly. He senses it, lowers his window. Generously he motions to me to come over to the car, making small talk about plans for the evening. He tells me he loves me, a blessing.

My own willingness to acknowledge my sadness without foisting it on him becomes a silent transmission of a sort, which he intuitively receives; it isn't cognitive. Knowing that he isn't responsible for my experience, we can connect deeply while maintaining our autonomy. And in calling me closer, his tenderness is a gift to us both.

We will continue this volley of care as he leaves for college, far beyond if we're lucky. His witnessing me opening to *myself* with tenderness in these seemingly inconsequential moments has altered something ancient within him; a quality of kindness and softness has begun suffusing our interactions during this most recent emergence into adulthood.

The question arises as I write to you: Might this opening to tenderness be a relevant practice for you? Offering compassion inwardly is a possibility for all of us, and we provide an example to those near us by practicing.

Does such a practice of tenderness with yourself hold meaning for you in this moment?

Who's offered their tender presence to you? What did it feel like to receive it?

Is there anyone in your life with whom you can practice prioritizing your autonomy to refresh the mutual respect you share?

Do you know anyone who seems to practice offering tenderness to themselves? How does that inspire you to be with yourself?

OPEN INTO IMPERMANENCE

Our practice is to welcome the passages of time, transfigurations of life, and shifting of roles—opening into what's next with clarity, with brightness.

Until I lost my mother, I couldn't imagine what death actually meant. I'd not yet experienced grieving consciously. I'd avoided grieving my grandparents, glossing over their deaths, numbing myself with schoolwork and addictions. During my mother's final moments, my left temple resting on her belly during her last breaths, my questions change: How does one *practice* grieving? How might I make peace with this pain?

During the week after her death, a dear teacher offers the insight that my pain and exhaustion are actually pathways for my body to heal, to be respected and treasured. I'd never encountered that perspective; I'd always been taught by example to power through, to move through grief efficiently and expeditiously. I'd always understood that to be strength, resiliency.

After learning that animals grieve naturally by resting for periods of time in solitude, I open to the truth that I need to pause and actually tend to myself in this moment. Being alone in the quiet predawn hours during the months after my mother's passing helps me see the end of her life as a beginning for my own, an empowerment of sorts, a new world of possibility. In those months, I open to the concept of impermanence—everything changes, my son will grow old, I will die—and everything becomes more meaningful, poignant, and rich. As a rush of creativity emerges, I find myself painting dozens of small-scale watercolors that will become the pages of my second book, a journal, fulfilling my mom's earliest desire for me. She'd always dreamt I would make art. Years later, catalyzed by that sadness, my practice of art-making continues, helping me work though confusion and pain as they inevitably arise, offering a release through the textures of emotion and color toward a more personal sense of peace.

What does grief mean to you in this season? Sometimes we're grieving the loss of a person, but often it's the loss of a dream, an idea, or a possibility. Sometimes it's the loss of a friendship. Accepting the inescapability of change can be the beginning of more ease.

What can this present moment teach you about impermanence?

Is there a certain ending or death that might be recontextualized as a beginning?

Could the death of an idea, a concept, or an experience be a door to something unforeseen and beneficial?

Can you practice offering your full respect, your attentive awareness to what's dying or changing?

2

Being Empty
and Still

Emptiness is a loaded, lonely word for many of us, containing connotations of weakness, loss, a void, and so on. Paradoxically, emptying my mind is precisely what I need to do prior to writing. Each time I return to this manuscript, it's best if I sit still first, drop my ideas about what's meant to come in next, and *allow*. Zazen is a helpful practice for emptying myself of intellectual ideation, making space for what needs to emerge. Emptying myself of the past, of identity, and of certainty. Emptying myself of doubt, of distraction, and even of insight quietly reveals a deeper peace. Being empty and still, I can ascertain what might be of service to our delicate, shared humanity.

EMPTY OF INSIGHT

What if emptiness is sacred ground, a place of *being* in which we can rest our assumptions, listen to the silence, and learn from the space around us? Practicing emptying ourselves of insight might reveal the stillness existing at the heart of all the strategies we employ to succeed, conquer, and grow. What if our practice of reflection is more healing than any insight we might be having?

As a graduate student in art education in my late twenties, I learned another meaning for emptiness—one that would return decades later to enliven my understanding of service.

Tutoring seven- to twelve-year-old children with their homework in the early evenings at the Abyssinian Baptist Church in Harlem, New York, I exit the subway in the darkening evening once a week all winter that year. I often pass by a closely huddled crew of five or six men with their hands over a fire in a trash can to keep warm.

Every visit to the church feels like a tender tug-of-war for the kids' attention. When I begin working with them, I have no idea that these hours are going to make an indelible imprint on *me* too. Over time, I learn my real mission: not to come with knowledge or insight but to come empty, open, and listening. I won't have the words until more than twenty years later for what I've come to know as the practice that serves best, in almost every context.

One of the first nights, sitting very still as I connect with a boy who needs help with his English assignment, I sense his need to build trust—in me and in himself—before he can write down his thoughts. Fearful that I'll do something wrong, I invite him to take out his pencil and paper, asking a few creative questions rather than jumping into an essay. He's visibly relieved, and so am I.

Asking him to identify sensations in his body and thoughts in his mind as he considers the impact of the work and life of Martin Luther King Jr., the topic for his short paper, he writes easily and swiftly, touching into a clear vision for his paper. From a few simple inquiries arises a thoughtfully crafted, layered piece of writing, about four hundred words, along with a sense of trust in himself. There was nothing to fear after all, for either of us.

The empty, open questions so often hold the answers. Releasing our fear, learning, and truly growing require us to arrive empty. To keep asking. The pages to come bring us to an empty field, where we can prioritize our questions instead of trying to come up with answers.

> *Like the bowl that has yet to be filled,*
> *there is an emptiness that precedes creativity*
> *that is alive with potential.*
> —TOKO-PA TURNER, *Belonging*

To serve others, we must let any fear of failure dissolve. We don't need to have stunning insights or perfect answers, only an earnest effort to serve and a willingness to let go of what we think we know. We can only enter into each situation certain of one truth: being empty opens us to learning.

In any situation that feels daunting, letting your fear of failure dissolve is an important bridge to connection. Emptying ourselves of what we *think* we know enables us to be less afraid of nebulous failure and to ask more questions instead of having answers.

What does emptiness mean for you in these times?

Where does emptiness show up in your life as a welcomed experience?

Where does it feel difficult to experience emptiness?

What gifts does emptiness hold for you, your work, or your relationships?

Have you ever let your fear of failure dissolve?
What was the result?

EMPTY OF THE PAST

So often we tell ourselves stories of our past as though they're happening today, ascribing value to long-gone occurrences that begin to seem more real than our present experience. We realize, in glimpses, that we can choose to continue running those films in our mind or acknowledge them and return to the present, as it is. We can get comfortable with reality when we question narratives, assumptions, and beliefs, when we let go of the stories from the past that seem so real.

For much of my adult life, I'd been longing for a closer bond with my younger sister. We'd both been holding on to stories in our minds about each other, unable to simply be *present* when we'd come together. It was always a bit fraught, tense, and unwieldy between us, sometimes erupting into real conflict.

When I was forty, I begin practicing softening the narrative around our relationship, rewriting the story of the two of us as I'd always *wished* we'd been. In my mind and heart, I start seeing us as trusting, laughing, close friends. This personal,

silent practice helps us. Timelines somehow began releasing; when I travel to see her, the new energy I'd practiced visualizing and writing down helps me to experience her—and *us*—differently. We feel more mutuality, sweetness. A decade later, she receives information about the medical issues with which she'd suffered as a child, knowledge that helps her talk to me about her early life, the facts about which I'd had no idea. She'd suffered greatly, which was kept from me. My parents felt this distance was in our best interest.

At long last we have the conversation I've always dreamt about. It isn't easy, but we manage it. Then I write a poem about it to help me process, giving temporary form to what was previously unsaid, relinquishing the memories and narratives of the past back into formlessness.

She feels seen by the poem, an acknowledgment of my desire and coexisting inability to bring comfort to her ailing body when she was small. Writing about how it was, then how I wish it had been as an alternate reality, I empty myself of the past and write a new story into being. And after several years of texting and talking, we finally meet; our hours together are relaxing and nurturing, at once new yet utterly familiar. A second poem emerges; this time, a haiku. It's called "Testament to Practice" and every time I read it, whether aloud or to myself, I weep.

> sister holds me tight
> our first hug, five decades in
> hiding tears of joy

The past can seem so real and present, causing an impact on reality as it is, when we continuously play the proverbial films of the past over and over in our consciousness. The invitation to be empty of the past is to come fresh to each circumstance, to release the familiar forms and memories back to their origins in formlessness.

In what realm of your life does the past seem to impact the present day?

Can you practice shifting the way you think and speak about a certain aspect of your past or a person in your past?

Specifically, can you soften the words you use to describe that past event or person, not to ignore or repress it/them but to practice highlighting the learnings gleaned instead of the conflict?

Might tenderizing the story expand your capacity to live with more ease?

EMPTY OF IDENTITY

Giving up the safety of our identity, we open ourselves to evolution. When we practice emptying ourselves of labels, assumptions, narratives, ideals, and even names, we can see and act from a novel vantage point.

At a few intervals across my adult life, I've received variations on this inquiry: How are you so willing to evolve? You've studied for years with several different teachers, honoring the currents of wisdom, then moving on when the time comes to move on. Are you not self-conscious about shifting gears? Do you not feel the need to explain things?

Entering into these questions, I feel a certain resistance that I've never exhibited outwardly. Every time I've shifted paths, detaching from a label, a teacher, a school, or certain teachings, there was discomfort, dread, and fear. Discovering instances when I'd given my power over to a narcissist, or diminished myself to be part of a group, I now see how important it was to override that resistance and press forward fearlessly toward my own evolution.

Emptying myself of identity has never been easy, but it's becoming a regular practice. I find myself disappearing now in certain moments, in meditation, in facilitation, amidst stands of trees . . . I feel expectations not my own slowly dissolving when I sit and listen. The practice of making myself available to what's true *right now* helps me see where I'm clutching onto name, form, or identity. Can I just be with what *is* again?

The gift of such emptiness is a new space in which to engage without self-deception and to be more fully present with the heart of my life and the lives of others. Whether I'm presencing my biggest mistakes, receiving a hug from someone I love, or cooking a simple meal, an unmistakable signature of patience is now quietly coursing through my emotional bloodstream. I'm able to see when it's time to move onward with less fear, more compassion, and less grasping.

The practice of sitting meditation is essentially a practice of emptying ourselves of identity. Tellingly, I fervently resisted meditation when I was attached to certain teachings, teachers, and ideologies.

What we are doing [in meditation practice] is having a taste of this One Mind: just plain, pure, clear Being. How do we come to this? Not by thinking about it, not by grabbing it, not by seeking after it; just by doing what the practice asks.
—MAURINE STUART, *Subtle Sound*

What does the practice ask of us? To sit quietly, to discern where we're grasping and when it's time to let go. And often, when we manage to practice, we begin seeing the various identities, the past and the future, as film sequences in our minds, eliciting chemical responses from deep within us. The practice asks us to empty ourselves of memories and identities that seem to take form as we sit in the silence, by watching them, breathing, becoming familiar with those opinions and beliefs, and returning to the land of the present, to reality just as it is.

Have you noticed the way the mind stirs up various ideas, visions, and memories whenever you're still, whether you're meditating or not?

Are there any identities—past, present, or future—that you're ready to release?

From where you stand today, can you imagine releasing the main facet of your identity that seems to best describe you at present?

EMPTY OF CERTAINTY

Certainty can be a liability; if I have an answer, the conversation ends. Asking more questions and practicing sitting quietly strips certainty away and allows a freshness to emerge, a bright curiosity. Sitting in stillness helps us hear the din and crackle of the thoughts that keep us busy, allowing us to prioritize the open spaces again. Concepts and narratives can fall away, we can venture out beyond self and other, beyond yes and no, dead and alive, right and wrong.

The first draft of this book—quote heavy and impersonal—is an earnest, enthusiastic gloss on my first three years of Zen study, mostly a well-curated collection of time-honored teachings that have little to do with my own personal experience. Anne Lamott's "shitty first draft" is the reality here.

In compiling those teachings, I manage to learn a great deal, but I gain even more perspective by emptying that file to begin again from the center of my being. Sitting quietly in the early mornings with nothing but a diminutive notebook, I set about recalling certain events in

my formation that've changed me. This isn't a comfortable enterprise, but the second draft slowly materializes.

Seeing the various projections, interpretations, and assumptions in my mind about a certain year or a persona I once prized, I can notice how these judgments continue impacting my choices right *now*. By emptying myself of those certainties each time I sit, little by little the inner landscape shifts. Some days I can sit with my discomfort and accept myself, even when I'm a ball of tightly wound hesitation and confusion. I can allow the yarn to unravel until I feel momentarily free again.

As I write these short personal essays to you, I realize each memory is a residue, a trace of an idea, a thread of some ideal, nothing to hold on to, no judgments needed. Yet each story holds information from the past that I am now tasked to learn from, then release. I feel more at ease relaying these missives without worrying how any of it will be received. My practice is to be empty of certainty. I simply don't know how it will unfold, which feels like freedom after a lifetime of seeking perfect grades and absolute answers.

Emptiness is present in every interaction and relationship, yet we humans still find ourselves imbuing the events of our lives with various levels of meaning. Imprinted and projected onto each moment are our attitude and our feelings; we can practice becoming aware of that process. Seemingly fleeting sensations can become fixed and immutable if we don't keep questioning.

Sometimes I still feel the emptiness of meditation practice as a challenge. Other times I catch glimpses of what it means to be nameless, formless, gone, free . . .

Empty of certainty. A release into simplicity. Emptiness is our invitation, and it's everywhere, awaiting our recognition.

Might you consider questioning and possibly releasing a certainty you hold dear?

Is there a situation where certainty—whether your own or someone else's—is preventing connection?

What concepts or perhaps relationships can be relinquished?

What does emptiness mean for you upon reading this?

EMPTY OF SELF-DOUBT

Have you ever found yourself in a job or a task for which you felt ill-prepared, but you took it on anyway, only to discover a capacity you'd never imagined possible? Self-doubt can stop us from experiencing the fullness of a relationship or an interaction, or it can point us to precisely the place of transformation within us.

Early in my son's life, a mother and daughter duo steal our hearts and become close friends of ours. Daughter Ella is in my son's kindergarten class, and mom Ruth works with me at an event and is instantly a kindred spirit. As the friendship deepens, I learn that these two are in a precarious situation. The most mundane aspects of daily life are unspeakably emotionally arduous for them.

We have the privilege of hosting them for a playdate most Wednesday afternoons, the one window of time each week when mother and child are legally allowed to be together. The rest of the time, Ella is in the other household, with Ruth's ex, who's basically gaming the family courts and committing serious crimes that will one day be addressed.

Hearing the ongoing updates regarding the abject wrongdoings is uncomfortable, but we do our best to make our time together calm and easeful for the kids. We make yummy food for the four of us, and we even let the kids watch shows on the iPad as we two adults try to make sense of what's happening. Which we cannot. But we keep trying. At the time of this writing, there are several cases pending that will hopefully expose the myriad bad actors, well over a decade later.

And almost every time we're together, toward the end of our few precious hours, we moms calmly sit on the edge of the bed in my son's room with both kids, and I gently ask Ella some important questions. First, I tell her that she can keep doing what she's doing, and she needn't look at me while I ask questions. It's fine if she answers in just one or two words. Ella assents, and she visibly appreciates just being *heard*.

Are you being physically hurt in any way? No.
Are you being yelled at? Yes.
Are you feeling safe at the other house? No.
Are you being treated with kindness? No.

Hearing her answers to these and other varied inquiries, I feel sad, angry, and afraid. Am I even the appropriate person to be asking these questions? I'm constantly uncertain as to how to proceed, but I continue the dialogue each week to help this child feel heard, validated, and seen. I don't offer advice, I just listen. I manage to stop doubting my capacities and just keep fortifying Ella's mom with friendship and presence. As Ruth is often representing herself in court, I offer to help with writing her legal responses and affidavits, learning skills I'd never have practiced, months of unpacking the seriousness of the situation to transmit what was needed.

Over the coming months and years, I witness Ella evolve into a beautiful, confident, strong, capable woman. She frees herself from the toxicity in the other household at the start of high school, learning to trust herself and eventually others, and escapes to live with her mother. At the time of this writing, she's got a full ride to college, and our fingers are crossed that all will get resolved.

Life presents us with endless choices—to doubt that we're capable enough, wise enough, or creative enough; or release that doubt and learn to trust ourselves implicitly. We're living in a world of too much visibility, too much information, and constant comparison. Witnessing our uncertainty and allowing it to consciously dissipate requires patience, gentleness, and care. I never know when doubt will show itself again, but I can see it when it's coming closer now, and I choose to trust myself rather than cowering in fear.

Can you name a situation in which self-trust has been elusive? Perhaps more than one?

Over the course of your life, who's helped you choose trust over doubt in yourself?

When you're plagued by self-doubt, what moves you to drop it, release it?

Can you leave your future self a few instructions for when you feel doubt creeping in?

EMPTY OF DISTRACTION

Once in a while, an irresistible invitation comes at just the right moment, summoning us to drop everything and enter into a new realm of discovery, to empty ourselves of every distraction and step into a new vision. Often the invitation is a harbinger of discomfort, asking us to change everything and come into a new relationship with the core of our lives.

I receive an email asking if I would be willing to lead a retreat in Bhutan and bring my family. The email arrives at a busy time when we're all drained from life in New York City. I've been building two businesses and dissolving a third. My son is in a new school, and my partner and I are entering into a committed relationship after significant external trials at the start. I am scared to walk away from everything for two weeks, but I am most certainly in. We all are.

○

We journey more than twenty-four hours to a tiny country tucked between Tibet, Nepal, and India. Arriving in Paro, in central Bhutan, we're greeted by an impossibly lush valley of tall green trees, winding trails, and palpable sanctity. We all fall in love immediately.

One of the first personal encounters we have is with Kinley, the woman who's been assigned to help us orient ourselves, keep our schedule, and ensure we have everything we need. No more than twenty years old, she is an absolute light, all smiling eyes full of sincerity. Instantly touched by her attentiveness, my son makes a new friend, and the two go off to explore and learn about the area around the house where we'll be staying. Her care is still referenced in our home; her kind attentiveness finds its way into our conversations to this day.

In this small but mighty green country, pristine forests and the quality of life rather than surging economic growth are the top priorities. Everything changes for us here. Bowing at altars in temples, walking silently up steep mountains with my hands behind my back, I feel a shift in my chemistry, my first taste of emptiness, and all distractions slowly begin to disappear.

Within a few days on the retreat, our group of ten has acclimated to the altitude (about eight thousand feet) as well as the much slower pace, and we are enjoying the local food and other customs. I share a few yoga and meditation classes, and several of us try our hand at archery practice. My son takes his first proper yoga class and during savasana, falls deeply asleep, comfortably.

Several of us hike up to a handful of temples near our accommodations, spinning prayer wheels and exploring ancient villages. Emptying ourselves of mental interference, we barely need to know how much longer we'll be walking or even where we're going. There's talking, to be sure, but for pockets of time on these walks, we move in silence, listening and breathing, our bodies receiving. What we don't know is that these shorter hikes are preparing us for a longer, more demanding and majestic outing to come later in the week.

In the midst of those forests, breathtaking birdsong is uninterrupted by any human noise. The quiet ways in which Kinley provides care for us teaches us volumes about how we want to mind ourselves for the rest of our days. In the evenings we watch Kurosawa films together and revel in his artistry, falling asleep as though in a dream within a dream. In this land, our family experiences moments of meaning and inexplicable dignity. Finding ourselves in an unforgettable territory of peace, emptied of distraction, we're changed at a cellular level.

Since that journey, I catch glimpses of a similar peacefulness in sitting meditation and while cooking, talking to a friend after missing her for a long stretch, and hugging my son when he lets me. It's there within and around us all, standing in line at the market this morning, in a hard conversation that needed to be had, even on hold with the insurance company. Empty of distraction, tasting hints of momentary, nurturing peace.

Has an ineffable sense of peace ever revealed itself to you in a moment of focus or adventure?

Is there anyone who offers you an example of this quiet ease, empty of distraction?

How does it feel when someone gives you their full, undivided attention?

Can you describe what unfolds within you when you're being heard and seen?

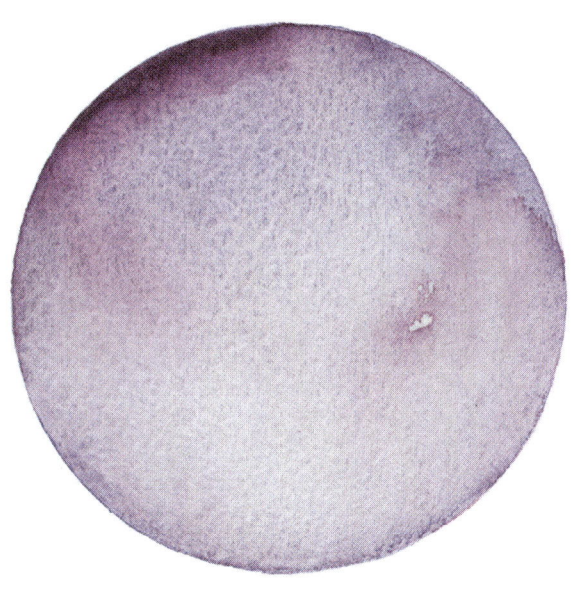

3

Bearing
Witness

◯

As we individually and collectively reckon with the human and environmental struggles of our world, bearing witness is a practice we can use to be with suffering and not be consumed by it. The reality is sobering; in every part of the world, divisions rage between individuals and communities, while formerly robust species struggle to survive. The best medicine we can offer is our practice of seeing others with compassionate, caring eyes.

Clarifying our own vision so we can bear witness to "the entire catastrophe," as one of my teachers often says, is an ongoing effort. Bearing witness with conscientiousness is a never-ending, ever-electrifying cultivation for us, when we choose to take it on.

SEEING WITH COMPASSION

Seeing ourselves with compassion helps us to guess what might best serve in any circumstance, no matter what pain we're personally managing. Our primary priority is to see ourselves with empathy, to bear witness and continue to acknowledge our own humanity.

Prior to studying nonviolent communication (NVC) with Judith Hanson Lasater, I'd drive my son to school each morning before he had his license and take his behavior personally. If he ignored me, I'd feel disgruntled and offended; if he was super warm and engaging, I'd feel safe and respected. At the mercy of the winds of change, reacting to the emotional roller coaster of a teenager with no discernible center to hold to, I'd feel unmoored several days a week, unclear on how to respond when he was in his own world, which was of course natural for a guy his age.

It's vital as parents to learn that our children are not responsible for our moods. When I needed to stop blaming him for acting his age but request respect, to be more patient with myself for feeling rattled when he needed more room to become himself, I found the practice of NVC to be good medicine for my parenting.

NVC practice teaches me how to acknowledge my humanity, and I am learning to observe my discomfort and offer myself empathy. Pairing NVC with my nascent experiences in sitting zazen enables me to identify new, peaceful pathways in the presence of swirling emotions. I can make an observation, determine what I'm feeling, ascertain what need isn't being met, and either offer myself empathy or make a respectful request.

This practice has changed the way we communicate in our family, especially in times of conflict, transforming our more challenging conversations into moments of steady support. Each moment of my son's evolution is a natural movement toward autonomy, of course. It takes me several months to crack the code, to not take his individuation personally, to learn how to simply ask for mutual respect. Paradoxically, over time, instead of assuming I need to find some way to connect with him no matter what, I'm learning to acknowledge when he needs space by offering myself silent empathy. Placing a hand on my heart, reminding myself of how human it is to be feeling this way, I feel seen, and the moment passes. How human of me it is to feel this way in *this* moment.

For more info on NVC, please see the resources section at the end of this book.

With this consistent practice, I can see when it isn't about me. My son and I have established a deepening mutual respect, and when I feel conflicted within, I offer myself this quiet, clear acknowledgment. I'm becoming the mom I've always wished to be, a support system with good boundaries, a pillar of safety able to bear witness to my son, while taking nothing personally.

Consciously seeing myself with compassion is my practice when it comes to parenting.

Is there any relationship in which you could be less reactive to external circumstances and clearer on where you stand in your heart?

In what current context are you being asked to see yourself with compassion?

When you practice acknowledging yourself with kindness when things are challenging, what changes?

YOUR VISION

Somehow, recognizing those who actively support my choices always leads to more support. Each time I've reached out to thank someone for their care, more is offered. When I first began cultivating a vision of true service, I found myself in an unusual situation—one that gave rise to a major shift in my vision years later.

Nervously entering my uncle's hospice room as a new mother in my late thirties, I steady myself by moving slowly. It's just Ben, my young adult cousin, and me in the room. Our mothers are my uncle's sisters.

Our uncle's body is significantly smaller than we've known. An imposing owner of businesses and keeper of secrets he'll never tell, we're both pretending to be unmoved by this deterioration. This is my first time being in close proximity to a body in the dying process; within a day he will expire. Somehow a burgeoning knowing emerges within me: I'm in sacred territory.

Sitting near his bed for several minutes, listening to his shallow, labored breathing, I allow myself to get quiet and trust that the right action will reveal itself to me. After some time, hesitation gives way to a sense of trust in the natural connection we've shared. An inscription in a book of Monet paintings he gifted me when I was a child suddenly warms my mind. Did it say something about trusting my heart and following my dreams? He was always such an energetic force—and he saw me for the person I am.

Ben sits next to me, just a teenager, holding space with maturity. Together we're unexpectedly witnessing the ending of this life and forming a bond that will become a close, enduring friendship.

Intuitively I begin practicing a form of energy work. From several inches above our uncle's resting form, my hands sweep the length of his body, vigorous movements to clear the energetic field of any residue of fear. When that naturally comes to a close, we allow several minutes of silence as we witness our uncle's body relax. We stand and say goodbye in our own ways, offer our respect, and make our way out of the hospice. A few years

from now, my cousin and I will recall with some incredulity the palpable feeling of release in that room. Our uncle passed one day later.

Decades since, this experience still fresh in my consciousness, I apply to a Buddhist chaplaincy program to learn and refine my capacity for bearing witness. Serving in a local women's shelter and a men's penitentiary prior to the program's commencement, I can see how unprepared I am as a child of Western society to bear witness to systemic structural violence, human sickness, and death. My studies have helped me see our historical aversion to these matters, but many years of on-the-ground experience are needed to give me the presence to quiet my mind, settle my heart, and see clearly what might serve.

I've been thinking with renewed interest how difficult it is to see or hear clearly. Settling the mind allows us to see things as they really are, relatively free of emotional or intellectual biases. Clear seeing may not happen the first time we sit, but maybe it will. Our chances increase with repeated sitting and continuous efforts to calm the mind. The question becomes, what is seeing clearly? What do we see? How do things actually exist?
—KATHERINE THANAS, *The Truth of This Life*

The support and encouragement I've received from friends and teachers alike have helped me confirm my choice to serve in this way. I can clearly see how being in service to the unsheltered, incarcerated, and dying will teach me to refine my care, patience, and listening.

What is your vision in these days, for your work, your service, your ways of relating?

Is there a certain aspect of your existence you can see but are afraid to see?

Who offers you precious acceptance and support of your vision?

Have their ways of seeing you shifted the ways in which you see yourself?

WITNESSING THE SELF

Seeing the entire scope of our experience with self-honesty is a practice in which we'll engage for our entire lives. How do we bear witness to ourselves at previous stages of our life without getting lost in the past?

I've been a meditation and yoga teacher since the age of twenty-eight, but in my early forties, I observe within myself a sense of self-cherishing, self-importance, that stops me in my tracks. Addicted to tobacco and marijuana, I'm now divorced, carrying a fair amount of shame, pretending I'm empowered and happy. Finding myself in a relationship that isn't as supportive as I'd hoped, I don't know how to exit calmly. I'm lost in small thinking and temper tantrums. Each day after I drop my son off at his school downtown, my long commute home becomes a sprawling, meandering, unproductive conversation with myself. And day after day I ask myself, *How can I get high as soon as possible without anyone knowing?*

Trying to make sense of the choice I'm making to get high every day, nothing feels nurturing except the time I spend with my little boy. Time is passing, and I'm struggling greatly. Spending much of my energy trying to do fulfilling work, I become convinced it's time to grow my reach, expand my business, and travel more. I pick up another business and engage with it fully. Social media emerges, and I jump in, sharing and creating. It all feels like too much, but I have no plan to get off the train. My way is unclear.

By some grace I begin an earnest effort at sitting meditation practice during this time, a time to bear witness to my many ongoing mistakes with some semblance of kindness. Even in shorter sittings, an intimacy with myself materializes, inviting me to see aspects of my painful, destructive, unintentional behavior. This consistent attempt to bear witness to myself becomes a foundation for more beneficial choices to come. At some point, my son's father and our lifelong sitter tell me they're seeing my damaging behavior, finding me challenging to work with.

They don't tell me what to do, even though I know they want to. With elegance, they hold up a mirror of sorts, encouraging me to consider ways to be more present and less afraid. I hear them, and a long and arduous process begins in which everything will change.

A decade later, a poem will reach me, typically chanted as a sutra in Soto Zen monasteries. "Song of the Jewel Mirror Awareness" is an arresting, paradoxical, and inviting piece. You can view the whole piece in the back matter on page 247. These lines remind me of that difficult talk, the gift of attention and truth from two people who care about me and my safety: "Practice invisibly, work intimately, / Be the fool with no voice."[1]

Upon first hearing it, I realize this was the invitation back when I was putting so much attention on "growth." This has *always* been the invitation: stop striving to be seen; instead, begin serving in a more meaningful way by disappearing into acts of service.

Practice invisibly. Sitting in the early mornings in the corner of my bedroom has become the most important connection of my day. What is it to be woven into the fabric of the present moment, without needing to be seen?

Work intimately. Staying close to myself, bearing witness, I can sometimes catch when I veer off and not abandon myself or shy away from what is difficult. Can you sense a fresh, foundational steadiness in your heart during conflict and change?

Be the fool with no voice. Spending much of my adult life seeking acknowledgment for my intelligence, silence has become my ally and ballast. Is there a relationship to silence you can craft to prioritize your own understanding?

Releasing our habitual strategies in favor of quiet patience, we infuse our lives with more connection, more kindness. We give ourselves and others a chance to feel safe in discomfort, less alone in unexpected pockets of silence.

Moving from activity to listening was a big leap for me. Busyness felt purposeful, growth felt encouraging. Realizing that I needed to practice shifting from doing and talking to listening was an awakening of sorts for me, one that continues unfurling and revealing more depth and clarity.

Historically, do you prioritize being heard or actively listening?

Where and with whom have you experienced quiet as eloquence? How did their quiet change you?

Where might you be numbing yourself or making yourself busy rather than witnessing yourself?

What is your relationship to silence in this season?

SEEING FROM WITHIN

Most of us aren't taught to offer ourselves emotional self-care when we need it; giving ourselves empathy is historically deemed selfish in our culture. Over time we realize that providing care to others from an empty cup is anemic, and we learn from experience how vital inward support is to maintaining our physical health and emotional resilience. As we learn to bear witness to ourselves, seeing from within is a crucial practice, a way to gauge and provide ourselves with the fortification we need to move forward, to serve.

For stretches of time in my childhood, as my parents are consumed with caring for my sister, I find ways to keep myself feeling seen in some way in smaller, liminal moments of my days: I gather my dolls, toys, sadnesses, and fears to create my own world of safety under my bed.

This is where I learn that I'm not a problem to be solved; I'm just in an environment fraught with challenges, and I deduce that the best way to help is to stay out of the way. And under my bed becomes my favorite safe place to do that.

Reading by flashlight to my dolls and toys, I find in books a collection of stories and ways of seeing to offer myself comfort, to feel safe in my small body. Growing more tender and aware of my surroundings as time wears on, I learn to see my circumstances and realities with clarity, kindness, and traces of hope.

Finding my voice in solitude, I begin to inwardly trust in the unfolding of this story rather than fear it. I spend an inordinate amount of time reorganizing my room, dusting off my Hello Kitty figurines to soothe myself, to bring order to things. Art makes its way into my life as my mother astutely provides me with a drafting table, art supplies, and a caddy to hold everything that feels so official. I begin drawing, sketching, painting, making greeting cards, barrettes, anything to keep my hands busy.

Confirmations come. My second grade teacher, dear Mrs. Petrilli, intuits that she can help me believe in myself and takes me under her wing. By sixth grade, Mrs. McGeough vivifies my creative inclinations by encouraging me to trust my art. In ninth grade, Mrs. Hochberg walks me into the world of watercolor and more philosophical ways of seeing art from both an additive standpoint and, more pivotally, a subtractive one (i.e., what does negative space mean in art-making?). Learning how to see what's *not* there in a work of art changes everything within me. Mrs. Hochberg takes us to the Whitney Museum of American Art in New York City as well as some smaller galleries, introducing us to working artists.

This real contact with the art world leads me inward, to begin seeing myself as an artist. As high school unfolds into university and beyond, art remains my primary lens through which to see, to know myself from within, with increasing respect and trust as time goes on. Over decades, I learn how to speak to myself about my work supportively and with care, which leads to more bravery.

Seeing from within isn't always easy or easeful. Looking back at several chapters of my adult life, I can see myself abandoning my own truth in favor of what's expected. Between instances of chasing mistaken notions of success to maintaining friendships lacking actual nurturance, moments of witnessing myself honestly from within shimmer at the edges of my awareness—reminders that I can trust the stillness. My chosen addictions were just coping mechanisms, cries for help, trying to feel safer, more seen.

At any stage of your life, were there coping mechanisms you employed that helped you feel safer or more comfortable?

What is the quality of your current inner dialogue with yourself?

Can there be more tenderness in the way you speak to yourself inwardly?

Is there anyone who's helped you to see yourself more clearly or to build more trust within you? Take some time and space to honor them, to thank them for their transmission.

ALL I CAN SEE

Certain experiences of quotidian moments open our eyes to what's true today.

I'm writing this while taking in a majestic view of South Guiones, looking toward Garza Beach in Guanacaste, Costa Rica. It's the middle of August, and the rainy season will soon take hold in this corner of the world. It's half past five in the morning; the birds, trees, and monkeys wake up, and the jungle around me is teeming with life. I can feel the presence of my mom here even though she passed years ago, particularly when I wake early. She loves being with me at this time of day when nobody and nothing else has my attention.

I find seeing clearly feels most natural when I'm taking in the details of my surroundings: The howler monkeys shouting to one another across the trees, waking up the entire forest. Sun playing on the tips of the leaves, the endless shades of green healing my eyes and lungs as I witness time passing, stopping, then passing again. The velvety slate color of the horizon today is turning silver before my eyes. Tree branches like veins seem to feed the entire planetary body. A bird with a blue-black plume is now poking her head above the mango leaves to see me, curious, completely free.

In this sixth decade of my life, witnessing has become a way of receiving, an uncomfortable freedom for a system long accustomed to being busy.

Committing to my quiet sitting practice, staying with it no matter how tempting it is to jump up and do something else, is a way to drop down into that freedom, allowing my small self to loosen its grip and slide away. The small self, longing to accomplish, can relax in such a state, but first, I actively allow the list of what I'm tending today to unfurl in my mind, slowly and with care, breathing as deeply as I can.

An expansive split-second silence opens before my mind begins conjuring thoughts again. When I was small, I thought I'd be a nun, a veterinarian, a clothing designer, an art teacher, a rabbi, a yoga teacher, an artist, and a writer. All the people I've been and might have become are suddenly present here, on this cushion. All I can see are

decades of personas, collapsing into one moment,
disappearing just as swiftly as they've arisen,
the most familiar strangers I've ever seen. Their
presence on this limpid, dampening, vibrant green
dawn in the jungle, so far from where I've last seen
them, brings a fleeting sense of recognition. Then
all I can see is the silvering sky again, flowing like
water, day breaking my heart open.

The following poem, "Nothing," is an homage to the
freedom I feel when I manage to allow the silence of the
morning to suffuse my field. Sparse language welcomes us
into a different stand of trees, the forest in New Mexico,
when thinking becomes superfluous and only the most vital
details remain.

nothing

tip of a leaf absorbing midday sunlight
this one waves at me,
tiny gem of aspen,
sounds of my mind forgetting
all the differences, targets, grievances
nothing left but light and drinking it

Is there anyone who's passed on who seems to "visit" with you in places you find healing? Do you find it easy to welcome their presence in?

Is there anywhere you find yourself bearing witness readily? Can you describe details of the sounds, scents, sights of such a place?

When you sit still, do any of your past selves tend to flicker in your consciousness?

Who or what did you think you *wanted* to be? Was it more than one thing?

Can you allow your mind to carry you into that possibility and back again?

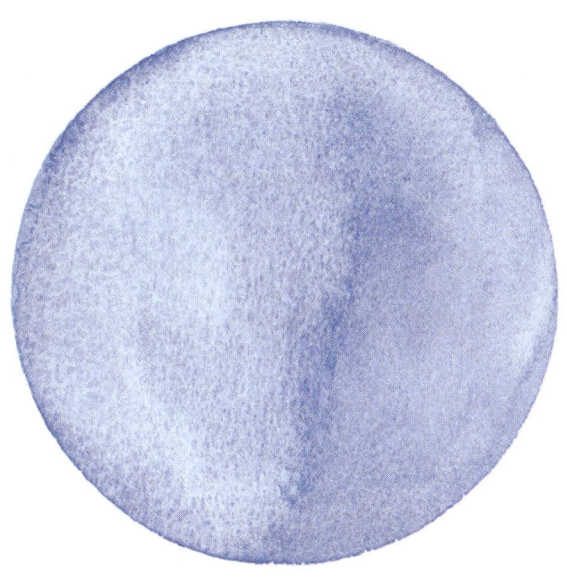

4
Taking
Action

In such fraught times, *action* is a loaded word. Mainstream media exposes us to countless iterations of conflict, heroism versus villainous behavior, losing versus winning. Opening this channel of listening in my life is shifting my definition of action, sweeping away my need to accomplish and achieve. In this chapter, we'll look at ways to redefine action and explore different ideas of action. We'll consider together the possibility that action can be a quieter endeavor than we've imagined.

NURTURING SILENCE

Practicing meditation in the early morning and some evenings, nurturing silence is the most caring action I can take, witnessing my heart widening into a new quality of attention. Ideas arise, difficulty appears, appreciation blooms, and a quality of internal strength reminds me to keep learning, growing, and offering the best of what I'm learning.

Many evenings of my childhood, I'm stationed at the top of the stairs praying for peace in my house. I almost never let them know I'm here—I want my parents to have their "privacy." I can feel the carpeting under my feet, my heart holding some notion that my peaceful, undetected presence will help them stop arguing. It's hard to listen. Somewhere in my young heart I promise myself that decades from now, I won't visit if they keep up their bickering. As a little girl of seven or eight in my flannel flowered nightgown, I learn the meager but real comfort of my own inner peace.

Sitting there, offering presence to my parents without telling them, I begin learning how to be with discomfort without solving or changing it, still a work in progress. This unintended silence practice from childhood has ferried me toward service, where my action is mostly listening: At the family shelter where I facilitate meditation to calm the frayed nerves of the women temporarily housed there. At the level two penitentiary where I guide yoga and meditation practice for the incarcerated gentlemen. In moments of attentive listening with my son's dearest friends.

These simple offerings of presence to those I'm serving are always somehow returned to me, multiplied exponentially. Aiming to serve with care, spaciousness, kindness, and efficacy, I try to bring my full attention and listening to what I'm doing. When the men laugh during yoga class, I include their laughter in the class. When a woman at the shelter picks up her phone mid-meditation, I invite her to come back whenever she's ready; no rush. When one of my son's friends needs to talk about something heavy, I practice active listening so that this human can feel heard. Invariably I leave these contexts feeling full, with active attention practice nurturing my *own* heart as well.

Spending time in meditation allows us to practice releasing thought-forms, letting go of narratives about how things ought to be, and returning to silence. When we open to these choices within ourselves, we can witness how thinking obscures our ease, then drop one thought at a time—seeing it, then setting it free—to return to the silence.

Does silence feel uncomfortable to you? Or can it feel nurturing?

What arises when you allow yourself to be fed by actively listening to someone else?

And are you able to sit and listen to yourself?

Can you recall a time when your intentional, attentive listening led to an unspoken healing?

Might you consider serving a population in your community in need of more listening?

EMPATHY

What if practice is not a path but an *expression*?

Whether through a practice of self-empathy, silent sitting, or quiet presence, our compassionate healing silence is an offering of our innate stability, a way we can take action in the world, and a foundation for the expression of peace we can bring to any circumstance or context.

As human beings, we habitually, consistently, even creatively avoid pain. Numbing myself with addictions to work, relationships, and substances, I've attempted to skirt emotional pain in several arenas. In my thirties and early forties, I disrespected myself by engaging in an intense roller coaster of drug use, resulting in destructive anger. Telling myself it was fine to smoke marijuana and lose myself for a few hours each morning, I'd come to believe I deserved this "break" from my life. Afternoon would come, I'd judge myself for choosing to get high and vow to stop, battling with myself and, often, with my family. This went on for several humbling years.

Becoming aware of my pain with a steady practice of empathy for myself, two specific practices help me relate inwardly with clarity and kindness. The first is meditation, which helps me illuminate, witness, and release the barrage of thoughts emerging every time I sit—thoughts of old pain, of future projection. Dropping each thought as it arises helps me see more clearly inside toward my own experience and outwardly toward the world.

The second practice, empathy, carries me into the realities of my life with clear eyes, an open heart, and a compassionate silence I'm sometimes able to offer. Judith Hanson Lasater shows me how to practice having empathy for myself, acknowledging sensations and being with my experiences without needing to change them.

How human of me, I repeat, day after day, whenever I feel grief, disconnection, confusion, or fear. Never losing its efficacy, the simple statement *How human of me* always helps me remember myself. Practicing this when I'm caught up in emotional story, I've learned to offer myself empathy in real time, helping myself move through charged moments with care and stability:

How human of me to create this drama for myself. How human of me to keep myself in this cycle of fear and frustration. How human of me to make that mistake. How human of me to doubt myself. How human of me to think the worst possible scenario is happening. How human of me.

Over time, this statement leads me to an important understanding: *I am the only one who can create pockets of safety within my own being.*

Landing in this silent understanding within myself, as I'm becoming a more attentive partner, a more consistently serene parent, and a better friend, I'm learning how to bring integrity to interactions and dignity to disagreements. The practice of silent self-empathy opens inner spaces I've never known, emptying me out, steadying me.

The following is an example of a silently spoken, inwardly focused sentence to offer myself empathy. Please use it as a template as you're experiencing things.

> *When _____ says/does _____, or When _____ happens, I feel sad, anxious, and irritated [insert your feelings here], because my needs for respect, courtesy, and connection [insert your needs here] aren't being met. How human of me to feel this way.*

In any uncomfortable scenario, by the time I've said this sentence within myself a second or third time, I remember: Each of us is having our own life, needs, and schedule, and yet we are inextricably connected. When I can feel empathy for myself, I can feel it for another, remembering that their behavior isn't about *me*. Everyone is having their own experience of forgetting our connectedness. Then, as if miraculously, I become a stabilizing, silent force for myself, *then* for the other, ceasing to take things personally.

Is there a time of day or particular context in which you could offer yourself just a few minutes of silent, vibrant recognition?

In what current situation(s) might you practice more self-empathy?

When you observe yourself being self-critical, can you practice acknowledging yourself with the statement *How human of me* and write a paragraph on how that feels?

WAVES OF LISTENING

Sometimes offering our open, unbiased, unfiltered awareness is the best kind of listening. When we practice deep listening rather than distracting ourselves or turning away, we can learn information to help us understand our people, our community, and our world.

One quiet winter night, my partner is almost asleep, and I lie down gently so as not to wake him. He stirs, then begins speaking. A story unfurls about the Mr. Spock doll he'd once found in the trash room of his building on Amsterdam Avenue in the 1970s.

"We couldn't afford such an expensive toy," he says, "so we'd go hunting in the trash room right after Christmas when the other kids would throw away their old toys, and I'd fix them."

My eyes fill with tears.

"I made Spock into a hockey goalie. I made a hockey stick out of an old eyeglass temple, which I put into his broken arm, and I carved goalie pads out of balsa wood, colored them in with magic markers, and sewed them onto his arms and legs. I made a plastic spoon into a goalie mask, and he was perfect."

Salty tears are streaming down my cheeks as I listen deeply.

"Then I made a goal out of a coat hanger and the plastic mesh from a Thanksgiving turkey."

I picture all of this, trying not to move at all, so his thoughts can keep flowing.

"And with the old hockey game, the one with the handles on the sides to control the players, I'd straighten out the handles so it would work. I would use popsicle sticks to replace the missing players."

I'm still silenced, heartbroken, hoping he'll keep going.

He turns to me and asks, "Does it make you sad that we couldn't afford the new toys?" An understandable question, given my tears.

"No," I say, reaching for his hand. "These are happy tears. It just means I'm lucky to have your heart and your creativity so near."

Listening is a matter of hearing beyond our assumptions, biases, filters, and imagination to an openness in which we release what we *think* we know, so we can respect what's *actually* happening. As some past iteration of me, upon hearing this story, I'd have felt sad, unnerved, and even awkward. In this offering of my listening, I learn about a layer of his being that makes my partner who he is: creative, scrappy, and deeply inventive.

What are some of the filters or biases that have stopped you from listening in the past?

With whom can you offer your active listening?

Without needing a certain result, how can you allow yourself to listen when what's being said might be hard to hear?

Name someone, perhaps a teacher or a friend, who's listened to you in a way that helped you know and appreciate yourself more fully.

LISTENING BEFORE SPEAKING

Deep listening is a practice of hearing with the heart, not from an agenda to be useful, witty, or smart. Observing our need to be heard rather than being present, intimate, and caring, we face the reality of our own suffering, which naturally leads to a protective sort of selfishness. This is a challenge for all humans on the path of service. May we stay open, engaged, and present.

The one yoga teacher training I ever offer becomes a training in listening for me, an ongoing unfolding of understanding that continues to this day. The training took place before I had a real practice of listening; as a result, I made several mistakes.

One day, a student in the training seems to be in emotional distress. Assuming that I'm being helpful, I call this person to the front of the room, inviting the rest of the class to offer love, supportive energy, and presence.

But I'm not actually *listening* to what's needed. I'm inaccurately presuming my role as the "teacher" in the room is to somehow *solve* this sadness for this person. If I'm honest, I also wanted to be seen and respected for my capacity to help. From my perspective today, as a student of council practice, I can own this moment as full of my own agenda rather than the timeline of the person I'd needed to respect.

If I could return to that moment today, I wouldn't disturb this person's healing with my ego-driven agenda to make things more comfortable—for myself or anyone else. I'd allow and accept the moment, trusting *their* healing to be an integral part of our *shared* healing. I would leave them be, and offer silent presence only.

Learning how to facilitate and hold space for various communities, I can see how natural it is to want to fix. Now I understand that individually and collectively, we are definitively in our own process, and our work is to offer respect.

Initiating this practice of listening, time and again I notice strong habit energy: to interrupt as soon as I sense I can be of some use. Realizing how much longing I'd had as a child to solve discord and make peace, to be approved of, to be seen, I can see how easily this habit energy continues to hold sway within me. Our minds are strong forces that yearn to interrupt any influx of new information. "I know about that" or "I can help with that" are, for some, natural and "helpful."

But listening before speaking is precisely what we're called to practice if we wish to be part of the conversations needed to bridge the deepening divides in our world.

Have you ever experienced disregard, neglect, or interruption at any point in your childhood or later, whether infrequently or chronically? What was that like?

Do you find yourself trying to solve or fix instead of listening? When and with whom are you most tempted to do that?

How might you learn from a deliberate practice of listening?

Is there someone with whom you could commit to practicing this?

LISTENING AS PRAYER

When listening becomes a form of prayer, our reverence reverberates. The state of surrender we invite when we disappear into listening is a balm for our nervous system and reminds us that we have the capacity to be with things as they are, present and willing to face what's here.

Visiting Bhutan remains one of the more formative experiences in the life of my family. Midweek during the journey, we trek to the Taktsang Palphug Monastery, also known as the Tiger's Nest, precariously perched on a sheer rock face almost two miles above the Paro Valley. The monastery is believed to be the place where the tantric master Guru Rinpoche landed on the back of a flying tigress, bringing Buddhism to Bhutan from Tibet.

The walk is at first a total delight: on a wide trail, pine forest air filling our lungs, and plenty of enriching conversation. Soon we arrive at a rest stop on the mountain, where the steepest part of the hike begins in earnest. Here there is an array of colorful fixed prayer wheels. Traced to Tibet in the fourth century, prayer wheels are ubiquitous in Bhutan, and it's common to find people of all ages spinning them while chanting mantras. Each wheel has mantras within and either painted or carved on the wheel, and spinning the wheel is equivalent to reciting the mantras.

Intended to relieve all living beings of misery, it's said that when the mantra is recited and the wheel is spun, enlightenment is shared with all sentient beings. Taking our time, we chant and consider the mantra our guides have offered: OM MANI PADME HUM. This mantra is meant to purify body, speech, and mind. I'm hearing it being chanted, and something within me keeps silent. Instead of praying to become different or new as I once did, the silence pervades my consciousness.

We walk on. As the well-trodden, ample trail becomes steep and narrow, my son tires, and our guide Norbu swiftly lifts him up onto his shoulders. The two disappear up the trail, engrossed in a chat, while the rest of us do our best to keep up. Passing streaming prayer flags at various intervals, we finally arrive at a rushing waterfall, at last seeing the Tiger's Nest emerge from a dense bank of clouds, a feat of human ingenuity seeming to hang off the slope. We enter, slowly, savoring the sanctity, our muffled footsteps being absorbed into ancient wood floors. The altar to Avalokiteshvara is where I find myself standing and lingering, while listening becomes the prayer I'm offering.

Losing myself in the fading colors, the hundreds of gifts and offerings, I've disappeared, am gone, intimately connected to a time and place I've never known. I don't move for some minutes; time has stopped. This place is reintroducing me to the prayerful silence I treasured as a child, leaving an indelible imprint on my heart.

Shifting our collective awareness from material wishes to simple presence, from industrial orientation to honoring the magnificent Earth and her wisdom, the energy in our world can shift. From the suffering we're witnessing as it echoes globally to the learning and deep engagement we're being asked to choose locally, our listening becomes more important as we become intimate with our own pain and that of others near us.

What pain or difficulty is currently present for you? You're invited to name it, to become more intimate with it, and to allow it to move through.

Is there anywhere you've been where your silence was your truest prayer?

What prayer(s) stood out for you as a child?

And if you could articulate a prayer for today, what would it sound like?

NO MORE TALKING HERE

Sometimes we hear news that changes our lives in an instant. And sometimes such information gives us a revitalized sense of what's important, what's really *here*. Most often, our capacity to discern the gift or lesson in painful news requires time in quiet, healing spaces where we can connect to the heart of the matter, so we can understand what's being asked of us.

Walking into the building on the corner of Sixty-Seventh and Madison, slightly nervous to see this healer again, the stoic young doorman sees me and wordlessly grins. He dials the house phone to let her know I'm here with one word: "Elena."

"Yes." I hear her whisper through the receiver.

I walk toward the elevator, and a hush falls over my mind as I prepare my energy for our encounter today. She's one of the only healers with whom I've worked whose very presence elicits a shift in my consciousness. The elevator rises; the doors open. Taking the few steps to her office as quietly as possible, I open the latch and set my things down in the corner of the tiny kitchen near the foyer as noiselessly as I can. In this office I've realized the value of silence, of caring presence. I don't want to make a sound.

Entering the main room, she sits on a low chair in front of the window, silhouetted. Her hand moves a strand of prayer beads, dangling from the edge of the chair, one bead at a time. She gestures with her hand for me to take a seat. It's been a few weeks since I've seen her, and we don't make idle conversation here. Even though we are also friends and she's been to my classes, I take a sip of water from the thin Moroccan glass she's left next to my chair and just wait for her to begin. Her eyes are patient as usual, but today something feels different.

Typically, after some moments of uncomfortable silence, she'd ask a few questions about my habitual overthinking, overdoing, rushing, or whatever self-sabotage I'm committing currently. Then I'd lie down on the table, and she'd begin: hands on my body, hands off, realigning, recalibrating my systems. I'd be transported to another plane, each visit a definitive shift. But today, as I look up, her eyes hold a composed stillness, a quiet depth where understanding and strength meet, carrying the weight of something known but not yet spoken.

She begins telling a personal story, speaking to me as her friend now. I'm surprised and thankful for her trust. While on a walk some days ago, she calmly shares, she'd felt some fluid around her heart and lungs, as though she was drowning. She went right to her doctor, and was rushed to the emergency room, where she learned she had cancer; the treatments would begin in the weeks to come. I'm trying to hold it together, not sure what to do or say, knowing how many women with cancer she's helped and supported. Then she invites me to get on the table like always, energy flowing through her hands more strongly and surely than ever.

The ensuing months of treatment, hospital visits from her close friends, moments of willing her body to produce certain cells and release others, confounding her doctors, will become a profound healing for her, for her children, for her friends and her patients. She continues silently teaching me from afar: anything is possible, all is given.

Looking back on these moments, I recall the sensation that washes over me when I witness any human skillfully turning their attention inward, moving with precision and gentleness, even in dire circumstances. I feel this in practice in the zendo, a sense of spaciousness, timelessness; ancient forms and intentions transmitted silently, no words required. The most profound teachings are intimately shared by example, in silence. Those examples continue to inform how I aim to be moving through the world.

Are there circumstances or relationships in your world calling you toward silence, where words aren't needed?

What have you gleaned from those wordless teachings?

Are you close to any people who are currently suffering, to whom you can offer your simple presence?

If so, practice being with them without fixing or solving, just offering your presence, then write about the smallest details of your sensory experience when you're practicing presence.

5

Grandmother's Heart

A fierce heart of tender listening, grandmother's heart is a cultivation in certain circles of Zen that carries equal measures of humility and compassionate presence. This heart is apparent in our choice to turn *toward* suffering, toward the difficult, and stay rooted in the ground of our being. Grandmother's heart trusts that we have the capacity to be present with whatever is happening, particularly in times of trouble. This heart is the energy at the source of our love, our practice, and our lives. "Equanimity and grandmother's heart protect us by giving us a base of support for the mass of our lives," writes Roshi Joan Halifax.[2]

When I consider the effect of this construct on my life, snapshots arise in my mind:

The plush green grass in my childhood front yard

The yellow lines unfurling under my bike's front wheel on our neighborhood streets

Wintry Cornell University campus, sideways snowfall, trudging to class in the trees

The bustling streets of New York City, the pavement beneath my feet

Art classes, especially bookbinding class at Cooper Union with my best friend

Countless yoga classes the world over—both as student and teacher

Our tiny secret wedding under the tree in Audubon Park, New Orleans

Our son being handed to me after I gave birth, the way my heart was broken and remade

My heart beating out of my chest as my mother takes her last breaths

Walking with my partner of the last decade on mountain trails through piñon and juniper, dusty red soil on our first backpacking trip, pitching our tent for the first time

Grandmother's heart has always lived within me, weaving itself into every one of these scenes.

CHOOSING TENDERNESS

Emerging from within us, grandmother's heart is a blend of ferocity and grace, unfurling as we grow older and more trusting. It's a subtle state of reverence in which pain is enveloped, and even the strongest grudge becomes a possibility for forgiveness.

In my first memory of Grandma Belle, she's at her house on Utterby Road in Malverne, New York, stationed on the couch near a rotary phone. While she's talking to a friend excitedly, her eyes beckon me to sit next to her, and I instantly feel like I'm being let in on a secret. Her hand waves vaguely to a dish of chalky pink mints that look like felted wool and taste like love. I devour two. The birch smell of those mints still comes to me in dreams when I know she's near.

About once a year, the damp, delicious scent of her outdoor walkway in Florida is my welcome into a week of being adored: plush peach carpeting, a slight tinge of mold in the air conditioning ducts, the cigarette smell wafting in from the terrace where she smokes . . . Each time I detect a hint of must or tobacco in hotel rooms now, I'll nostalgically recall this place as one I've called home.

We eat breakfast every morning at their tiny wrought iron–and-glass table in the kitchen. A perfectly toasted sesame bagel with cream cheese, bowl of cottage cheese, and cup and saucer of coffee on the side, watching *The Price Is Right* or *Family Feud* on a television no bigger than my hand. Scotch-taped reminders on the kitchen sink backsplash—to take these pills, to call this friend—and on the counter, her pill bottles and her Benson & Hedges cigarettes. I revel in her gossipy phone chats with her friends even though I never really know what she's talking about.

We take walks down to the small pool at the back of the building; the one that used to be scary and huge to me when I was very young, the one where I first realized I could swim. Each year as we take the elevator down there, I'll notice that I'm supporting her arm a bit more. I grow; she shrinks.

My grandfather Papa Carl, her husband, is my hero. Tall, silver-haired, handsome, and confident, he takes daily naps in his recliner, teaching me that rest is an expected feature of the schedule here. They spend their days arguing then making up, just like my parents.

One day in the future, as a reaction to this bickering, I'll learn to prioritize mutual respect in my primary relationship.

When Papa dies during my freshman year of college, I find my way back to that apartment for what will be one of the last times. I rub her feet every afternoon while she rests and says, "Oh, *Elena*, thank you," over and over. I can feel her deep sadness in my own body. She lets me sleep in his bed, next to her, and I hold her hand as she falls asleep each night. This is the first time I'm taking full care of her; everything's changed.

One afternoon I finish a yoga practice, leaving my mat on the floor in her living room to go for a run. While I'm gone, Grandma Belle trips on it, hitting her head and breaking her hip. I receive a call from a relative; Grandma Belle's in trouble. I return to a pool of blood on the floor where her head has hit the tile. She's already been loaded onto a stretcher when I arrive; I'm ushered swiftly into the ambulance's passenger side and whisked to a nearby hospital where one of my childhood friends, by some coincidence, is tending to her. My grandmother forgives me instantly, decades before I'll be able to forgive myself. In a few short years, she'll fall ill, unable to sustain herself with this injury and her lonely, broken heart.

She asks for me the night she dies, but I'll never know what those words sounded like; I was a thirty-something girl on a numbing mission and didn't show up for her final days. Never again will I resist the presence of death; I will walk toward it. Her death, then my mother's, have become the scaffolding around my own grandmother's heart, my heart of acceptance.

Years later I'll be hired to teach at a festival in upstate New York, at the summer camp where my grandparents met for the first time, where my mother spent several childhood summers. A healing happens in my heart there, more quiet mercy arriving in a dream on night one in which Gramma Belle holds my hand and repeats that phrase again and again: "Oh, *Elena*, thank you."

Grandmother's heart is a willingness to be intimate with reality, to let circumstances render us more tender, caring, and present. In time, with practice, grandmother's heart becomes the softest place to land within ourselves.

When have you felt the energy of grandmother's heart alive in you?

Have you ever made a choice in which you've denied your tender grandmother's heart?

Can you offer your grandmother's heart to any mistakes you've made in the past?

Who has offered you their grandmother's heart over the course of your formation?

YOUR HEART'S RITUALS

Unprescribed, unplanned rituals of the heart connect us to moments of care—for ourselves, those with whom we come into contact, and our world. Allowing yourself to create nurturing rituals and practices of your own to honor what you're working on becomes natural. Rituals can be instrumental in stewarding yourself through hard times. As you consider rituals for yourself, take care to discern the difference between supporting yourself and hiding from yourself.

When people ask me how life as the mother of teenager is going, I usually feel a warm burst of love, a bone-deep thankfulness with a peppering of humor regarding my many failures in raising this human. I've spent his life crafting both personal rituals and practices of connection, conversation, and care with him. He's now a grown man, with rituals of his own.

Around the time my son turns three years old, a friend teaches me to take time each evening to ask him what I could have done better that day. Nightly at bedtime, this ritual teaches him that he can safely share his discomfort when my behavior doesn't feel helpful or kind to him.

This ritual also teaches us the gift of mutual trust: I listen intently, thank him for the feedback without defending myself, then do my best to incorporate his thoughts in the coming days. I trust him to be honest, and he counts on me to transform my behavior. These conversations help to create a trusting yet discerning soul with a kind way of moving through the world, and I can detect a burgeoning sense of compassion in him, a knowing that everyone is just doing their best.

From the vantage point of now, I can see that time was when I began touching into this quality of grandmother's heart within myself, a contributing factor to my comfort with growing older. Threading through the years, this ritual is useful in other contexts, providing me with many chances to become an active listener willing to learn from my many errors.

◯

From that time on, over the ensuing few years, I struggle within myself, toggling back and forth between the clarity I share with him in the evening hours and my muddled, addicted mind that haunts my days.

Mornings after dropping my son at school, I'm smoking weed daily, cleaning aimlessly, then sobering up to teach. Observing this happen day after day, promising myself to end this charade, one day finds me rationalizing my behavior to a sober friend, who relays the words that change everything: "You cannot *possibly* do the work you intend to do when you're getting high every day."

Within weeks of hearing her words, I close the door on my addictions, pointing my compass in the direction of self-acceptance, and begin feeling my feelings again. Clarity feels like a priceless gift, especially when life feels painful. For some months after I begin my sober journey, it feels like my organs are releasing the numbing compounds I've been taking in, and a vexing anger is a ready presence. I spend those months seeking and finding the tools to make sense of the rage as it passes. Art becomes my ritual of observation and healing, but meditation helps me turn the page.

In my bedroom I create an altar at the foot of my bed on a low table, placing on it a small watercolor painting, a felt cloth under a tiny vase of flowers, and a candle. I begin practicing sitting meditation seated in front of it, noticing tendencies, inner tantrums, and worries about failures and future. Some days are more excruciating than others, and I begin cultivating responsiveness—toward myself and with my family in times of conflict, especially when I've been the source of it.

As a ritual to help me stay grounded in grandmother's heart, sitting is where I practice bringing this quality of being to the foreground, offering myself words of support, as my own grandmother would when I needed her comfort most. During this initial interval in my recovery, I find ways to express the tiniest incidences of self-acknowledgment. And in the same hall closet where I once kept my secret stash, I begin storing my watercolor paints and go there after each sitting to create the small paintings that will be the precursor to the book you hold in your hands.

Especially when circumstances seem overwhelming, turning our attention inward helps us to observe the mechanisms of discursive thinking—the inner dialogues that keep us from connecting to our innate wisdom. If it's challenging to practice sitting in silence, begin at the beginning with three deep breaths. Sitting meditation, also known as *zazen*, even when practiced by only one person in a household, has the capacity to usher a whole household or community into a new experience of kindness. One person turning on the light within can move mountains. A reminder that simple meditation instructions are located in the backmatter on page 245.

Here are some other practices I've chosen to do for certain periods of time:

- Practicing yoga nidra via books or recordings

- Choosing a card from a favorite deck of prompts or words to offer direction

- Offering myself Reiki upon waking, simple hands on heart and belly, inviting the body's innate preference for homeostasis, for balance to take over for a few minutes

- Putting my legs up the wall for a lymphatic reset

- Walking outdoors early in the morning

What are ways you can connect to grandmother's heart within you?

What are the rituals that support your healing heart?

Are there any practices you'd love to finally invite into your life?

Might this be a moment to reinstate a practice you left behind some time ago, to welcome yourself back to it with humility, commitment, gentleness, and precision? If so, how? Be as specific as you can, so you can look back on these notes for direction and encouragement.

GARDEN OF EMPTINESS

Grandmother's heart shows up as I cultivate my first vegetable garden, applying the tending lessons of emptiness and spaciousness to other aspects of my life.

When we move to the southwestern high desert from the deep man-made canyons of New York City, I inherit a raised-bed garden, overgrown with mint, strawberries, and weeds. I clear the small space and begin learning about this tiny field of potential in which anything can happen. I begin asking questions.

Which vegetables do well at this altitude? How many seeds are needed per inch? How deeply do I sow each seed? What do I need to do as they grow—thin them out, give them space? I'm learning a great deal about the difference between *intervention* and *allowing* in my first year of growing. I apply these lessons to my parenting and partnering: interfere less, value the inherency of emptiness. No need to know or control how it will turn out. Allow things to be as they are.

These teachings become expressions of my own grandmother's heart as well, and give rise to more questions.

How spacious can I be with my son to allow him to become himself? How much room can I offer my partner as he adapts to his surroundings after an entire life in a big, bustling city, to acknowledge the possibilities for his biggest ideas to be made real?

During the first growing season, I learn that certain herbs and veggies thrive here: parsley, radishes, beets, spicy arugula, lettuces, and spinach. Earlier planting and tending makes way for a possible second round in late summer. When I neglect to thin out the early growth to make the space the plants need to flourish, the ensuing tangle makes harvesting more difficult.

Emptiness is everything, it seems, even in gardening.

In late July, I experiment. I plant a few dedicated arugula seeds super thoughtfully to see if we might be able to enjoy some giant, spicy leaves in September. The leaves on each of these ten plants have become as big as half my forearm, with a spiciness that still surprises us.

Silence and space are required for us to evolve. In emptiness, we have no fixed idea or assumption of how things are or how they *should* be. In emptiness, we practice accepting precisely what is and how to work with reality.

Consider your heart: a hollow, muscular organ in the center of your chest about the size of a closed fist; an empty space from which freshly oxygenated blood flows to all parts of the body freely with each heartbeat. The example of the heart is pivotal for me: *all nurturance flows through here; practice staying open and empty.*

How can I become more like this? Can I make my life into a place through which nurturance flows freely?

> *We usually perceive things in a dualistic way by separating ourselves from them. Then a gap appears, which makes room for anger, ignorance and the various other ideas and emotions that disturb us. But when we really make ourselves empty and realize that everything is nothing but the self, the gap is eliminated, and we see phenomena as they are.*
> —TAIZAN MAEZUMI AND
> BERNIE GLASSMAN, *On Zen Practice*

Have you experienced the wisdom of making space to allow for a being or project to thrive?

Attached to nothing, can you allow experiences, loves, losses, and painful moments equally to pass through?

Does the heart's inherent emptiness hold wisdom for you?

Describe an incidence of making space, for yourself or another, inviting emptiness to be your teacher.

OUR EVOLVING
DEFINITION OF FAMILY

Learning to see ourselves clearly with a loving and open heart helps us be caring with ourselves in times of confusion and grief. And sometimes we need the support of family—so evolving our definition of family is important.

When I close my eyes and think "childhood," within the first few memories my mind cycles to the dining room table at holiday time. Around the table I see my mother's parents, along with her siblings in various configurations, and their children. The tidal swell of the family, everyone alive, young, relatively healthy, feels comforting to me. But the incessant cigarette smoke makes it hard for me to breathe.

The caustic interactions between the adults begin unfolding within minutes of being seated, and I feel sadness in my small body. Ridicule is lobbed freely across the table. No moment is sacred; respect is nonexistent—or so it seems to me. These adults all *say* they love each other. "We can make fun of each other because we're *family*," my mother tells me when I protest. My body tells me otherwise.

Unable to hold the rift between their concept of love and my own, I disappear to my room as soon as I'm permitted. How can they treat each other like this? How can this sharp-tongued meanness possibly mean "I love you"? Two decades later, fault lines will grow into vast chasms between them, their conflicts and estrangements to be buried with them as their lives come to a close.

Confused and without much guidance, my future relationships will be laced with, and informed by, this paradox. For years, volatility, inconsistency, and insecurity will reign as coping mechanisms for me in my partnerships, leading me to a handful of therapists throughout my adulthood and hundreds of hours in meditation practice, learning to befriend my mind.

Forty-plus years later, my eight-year-old self still needs reminders that her intuition is sound, the safety of solitude in her room is sometimes warranted, and she can trust herself to know what's needed next.

Family includes *all* our relations. It's not confined to our blood family. It's our *people*. Our humans. Our community.

My family consists of the friends I made in the 1990s while finding my way in New York City. It includes my university friends, cemented by an ongoing text thread of birthday wishes, memes, and pictures of children attending our alma mater; and my camp friends, together for a decade in our formative years, when we found ourselves learning how to take care of each other for a couple of months every year. It also includes the people with whom I trained to teach yoga, and my meditation friends with whom I sit in silence.

Those I met virtually during the pandemic, some of whom I've never met in person but with whom I've shared the depths of despair, are also my family. As are my dearest, closest humans, the ones who live near us and farther afield, the first ones I call when something in my life goes awry. Family is also my sister, my dad, my son's father.

These are *all* my relations.

Reaching out to check in, trusting that when I think of them, it's the right moment. Silent mornings having tea on my living room floor, long phone chats from the road, gifts of skin care products and bags of clothes, picnic-table lunch dates, handwritten cards, volunteer hours, fancy dinners, and sending my son random unexpected baby pictures. These are ways in which I uphold and nurture my relations.

Sharing space, sending care, showing up, listening well . . . how do you nurture your relations?

Are there any relations with whom you could practice being more attentive, creative, and present? Name them and remind yourself of some ways you could do this.

From whom have you been offered attention in these ways? How has that care changed you?

THE LOVE
SURROUNDING YOU

In our times of deep divisiveness, laced with generations of dehumanization and marginalization, our shared integrity is consistently challenged. We all know this to some degree, and our willingness to see it and admit our role is an expression of our grandmother's heart in action, crucial to our collective healing.

When I meet Brian Francis, also known as White Bear, I feel an instant sense of kinship. Brian is from the Mi'kmaq Nation (pronounced MIKmaw) of New Brunswick in northeastern Canada. Brian's writing, art, and steadfast friendship provide a safe landing, as well as a firsthand perspective on the prolonged experience of being marginalized and dehumanized since he was a child. His art and writing are reflective of his willingness to begin again, to forgive, walking us all closer to Spirit with consistent respect. He reminds us to offer our care to Nature and her mysterious beauty. His forgiveness makes an indelible impression upon me.

In his book *Between Two Worlds: Spiritual Writings and Photographs*, Brian implores us:

> We must remain humble, loving, caring and sincere in order for us to hear the teachings within our hearts.
>
> Set aside the ego and look beyond to see the beauty of Creation all around.
>
> All was created for us while here on our medicine walk. Let us be open to receive the love that surrounds us.[3]

One of Brian's gifts to me is a simple greeting offered during one of our meandering, nurturing phone calls. In his tradition, when a ceremony has come to an end, a prayer is said: *"Emset nogemag,"* meaning "All my relations."

This acknowledges the ancestors who've passed on—honoring "every one of them since the beginning." They are each who we are today. Those who've come before us make us who we are.

Brian opens this portal of respect, so I can honor every single ancestor of mine with one breath, one moment of consciousness, even though they fought mercilessly around the table, showed up in conflicting ways, gave mixed messages. Substantively shifting how I show up, Brian's understanding is changing the words I use, the care with which I move, and the ways in which I bring my heart to those who show me love.

We're asked to care deeply for our internal experience, so we can care for others. We're asked to stop objectifying fellow living beings, to cease dehumanizing people with whom we don't agree. We're called to create contexts of kinship, connection, and community.

The word *kinship* is more than a word; it's a gesture, a feeling, a state of being . . . one more layer. To remember that we belong to each other is to turn our attention toward our integral interdependence, bringing us back into relationality with our Earth and with each other. From this remembrance, we feel gratitude, humility, connection, and even grace in the face of the vastness. Of course, there are those with whom we feel we don't align—it's difficult to imagine how we coincide. And yet, this is our task.

We come from the same inconceivable source, the same marrow, the same impossibly detailed vessel, with the same heart cells. When we can acknowledge that, we feel ourselves steeped in recognition, inside of which we can be a good friend, a caring presence for someone who needs it.

Honor those with whom you share space and time, both the ones with whom you find yourself struggling and those who show you love.

Making a list of their names, perhaps you might elucidate ways in which their offering to you has transformed the way you see yourself.

Might you find kinship with anyone with whom you don't agree?

Is there a way in which you can acknowledge ancestors with whom you don't feel aligned?

Can that recognition be a way to locate appreciation for your own perceived shortcomings?

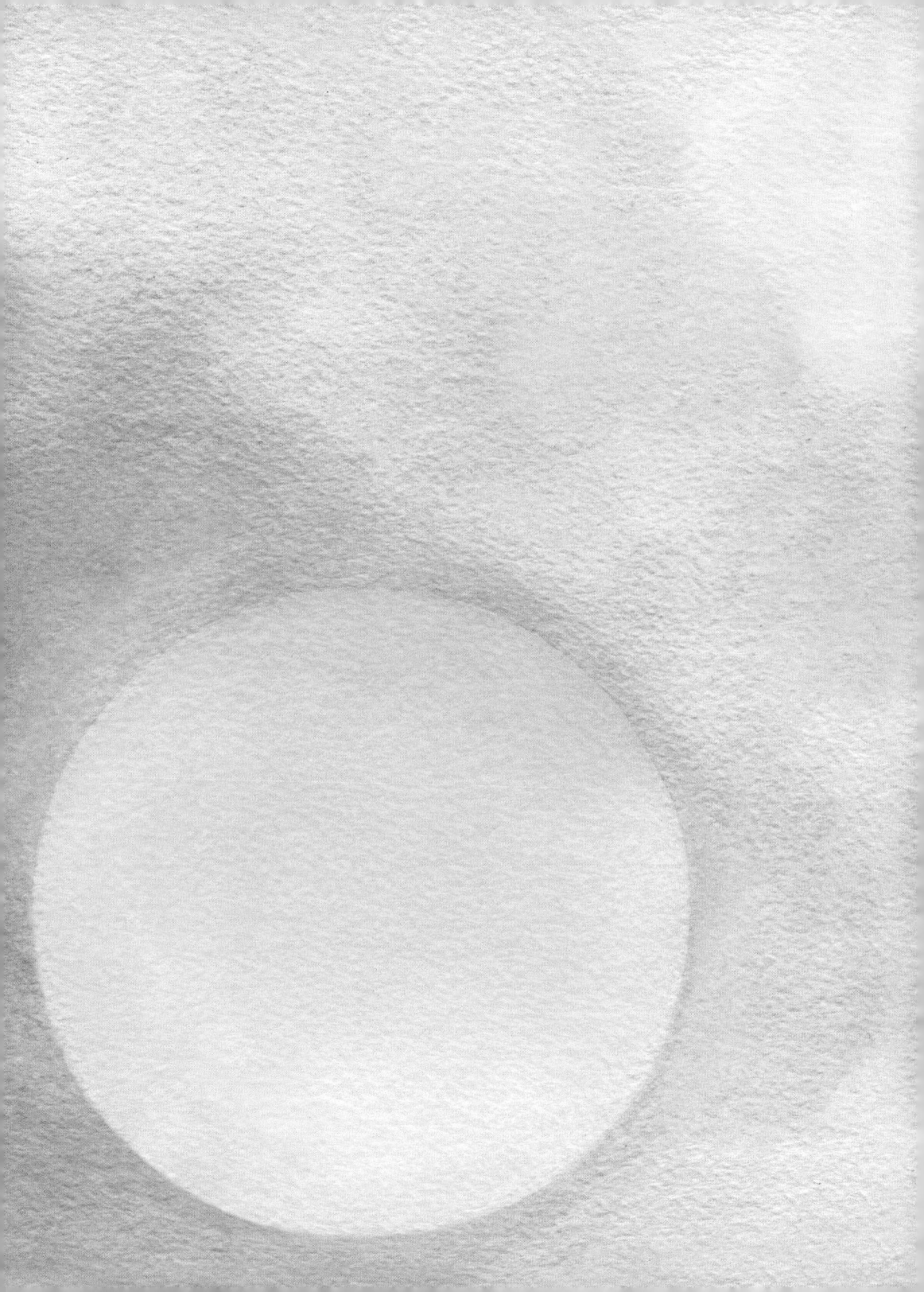

6
Opening
to Stability

As we learn to be present for reality as it is, we grow our willingness to make room for dissonance, even while holding steady compassion. This spaciousness opens to the solid ground at the heart of every situation. Opening yourself to the stabilizing principle at the center of every circumstance is a choice, even when there is confusion and pain.

Especially then.

BRAVERY AND INTENTIONALITY

Bravely facing what feels daunting, while honoring our intentions, is an ongoing practice. I keep asking myself this question: *Is my intention informing this matter, or is my original objective obstructed?* No matter what's at stake, holding clear intentionality close gives us the courage needed to face what's next.

As I become the parent of a thirteen-year-old and the mother of the Bar Mitzvah, the voices of our family in prayer are rising up from every corner of this synagogue in downtown New York. Catching my father's eyes in this moment, I'm missing my mother in a way I couldn't have imagined. Tears are falling, closest friends are beaming their love at us from the audience, and hope is in the air, feeding each of us.

That evening finds us in my former partner's home uptown for a glorious celebration; our boy becomes a man in the company of close family and friends. The completion and commencement are evident in my son's smile as he engages; this feels like the beginning of an important stage. We have no way of knowing that within a few short months our lives will be unrecognizably altered by a global pandemic.

Within five months we're moving to the Southwest with a handful of friends, innumerable hiking trails, and the scents of sage, piñon, and juniper. We spot the Upaya Zen Center on our way to a hike on day two. Abbot Roshi Joan Halifax had made an indelible impression on me decades earlier in New York City—now I'm slowly driving past the school she's founded, one mile from our new home, about to steep myself in her work of living with care and dying with consciousness.

Since Upaya is closed due to the pandemic, I become a member and begin by taking as many virtual courses as I can, including longer practice periods, weekend intensives, and meditations. Cozy corners of our rental home become quiet spaces for meditation as learning takes center stage, and my partner and son support this time in which I learn how to listen and change. I dial back my other work to place myself in the path of

Soto Zen. Through the work of Roshi Joan and other teachers at Upaya, the practice of opening to my inward stability becomes a priority. Daily sits, weekly volunteer shifts, and baking for the unsheltered lead to a level of inward fulfillment and connection I've never imagined.

Over eighty years young, Roshi Joan Halifax holds a combination of bravery and intentionality, gravity and compassion. Her commitment to continue serving, to help us find acceptance amidst grief and pain, is a beacon. Coming closer to her anthropological mind, her activist heart, and her life of service, I'm enriched, softened, strengthened, and transformed. In small increments, the way I conduct myself within my family, in my community, and within my own being has begun to shift.

As I continue sitting and hearing several teachers at Upaya speak, an understanding of bravery emerges: it is our willingness to be with reality. This willingness is in evidence when we choose to adapt in the face of inconvenient truths, when we listen well when challenged, and when we accept that sometimes we won't know what to do when we feel out of balance. Bravery requires awareness of both your internal state *and* your external environment.

This is an ongoing engagement.

Whether you're caring for an elder, a child, a sibling, a partner, or yourself, bravery and intentionality weave together in the fabric of your being, ensuring you take care of yourself if you wish to keep fortifying and uplifting those in your sphere of care. For me, bravely prioritizing my practice of meditation is how I uphold my intention to serve in my volunteer placements. I cannot keep giving without resourcing myself.

How do bravery and intentionality intersect in your being in these days?

How do you practice facing what's difficult in your work, your householding?

In what realm of your experience are you able to compassionately listen? Are there any relationships in which it's especially challenging to be attentive?

What does your service look like in this time of your life?

A PRACTICE OF PRAYER

While we naturally long to feel safe and steady, we know it's also our task to be comfortable with not knowing, to live with uncertainty. As I grow older, I'm practicing silence and stability, curating circumstances within and around me that feel safe. Pouring tea, sitting still, walking in the trees—quiet, wordless acts of prayer bring nurturance and safety. From these silences, words of prayer arrive in my consciousness, and I'm no longer hesitant to express them.

Walking onto the black sand beach in Playa Ostional in Costa Rica at dusk, clouds collecting just above the horizon, I'm cautiously following our guide down to the shore as he repeats multiple times that we must stay together. Unavoidably I drift, lost in my heart, incredulous at what I'm seeing in front of me.

Moving cautiously, thousands of olive ridley sea turtles have come to this beach to create their nests, lay their eggs, and fall into a meditative trance before taking to the water once again. My only aim is to offer them a broad berth. Tears are unexpectedly streaming down my face.

Each turtle mother lumbers gracefully up the beach and finds her place and begins digging with her hind flippers a hole deep enough to lay seventy to eighty eggs. All of this happens as though in slow motion; I wish I could better explain it. Having spent most of his life caring for these beings, our guide reaches gently under the turtle I'm following to gingerly move some sand, inviting me to bear witness as she lays dozens of eggs. I feel unsteady watching her private, sacred act; a fellow mother.

Her body convulses in a cataclysm of giving. Eggs fall quietly into the hole a few at a time; more tears fall down my cheeks. Something about the Earth's majesty and the holiness of what I'm seeing emerges from within, a prayer of wholeness, appreciation.

I don't move for thirty minutes; she completes her mission and goes quiet, this pulsation from life giving to rest. A question arises next, my heart bursting out of my chest as the chill of dusk falls over us. How do they know where to come, what to do, with such precision?

Closing my eyes alongside her as she slumbers, sixteen years peel away, and I can smell my son's newborn head as the nurse hands me this tiny six-pound parcel of life for the first time. I can feel his weight as I take him into my arms. I can hear the small sounds he makes as we meet again, he in this new form, outside of me.

Wishing for stability in this unrelenting mystery, more words emerge from my silence on this black beach: *May these hatchlings survive, and may we all find peace in our places. May we be well and safe. May we be happy. May all who suffer find ease.*

With these words, a wash of softness falls over me along with the impending dark of the evening. Our guide calls us back together; it's time to leave. I see the faces of my friends coming nearer, all awestruck, similarly moved to tears.

What is the purpose of prayer, after all? Is it to move past my own impulse toward self-preservation so I can serve others? Prayer seems to me the most natural, spontaneous, unprescribed way to affirm what's here, to ask for the ever-elusive stability for which we ache on certain days. Prayers reflect our willingness to remain available to what's present, to be open to what's happening so we can respond appropriately.

At the end of each meditation or yoga practice, I dedicate the merit of the practice to all beings, asking for the health, happiness, and safety of all, in all realms. Each of these dedications is a prayer, a way to reflect on the paradox of what's unfolding.

To what simple majesties are you privy in these days, in your friendships, your alliances, your work, or your play?

What is your prayer for today? Might you craft a prayer to acknowledge something simple in your space?

For example, my impromptu prayer of gratitude for this moment: *Thank you, Mother Earth, for the bounty you offer me as I tread as lightly as I can. Thank you for the chance to express myself and heal in the process. And thank you to my best friend for offering me the intimacy of her presence as I'm navigating a trying time, especially her clear invitation to just be myself in her midst.*

PRAYING FOR SOFTNESS

Our stories are marked by incidences of presence. Cultivating our capacity for acceptance in the face of any arduous reality, we find our way toward softness and ease, both in our behavior and our relations. And sometimes praying for that softness can help us move toward the transformation we seek.

Our friendship begins as adults in our thirties. The moment we meet, she leans in with familiarity and fearlessness, smelling my neck, smiling ear to ear. We're checking in for a weeklong retreat on a mountaintop in southern Utah, nine thousand feet above sea level, and I love her already. My new friend.

Hours are spent in deep late-night talks and early-morning canyon dog walks. Mats next to one another at classes all over Los Angeles during the height of everything yoga would eventually become.

Creation energy perfumes our friendship through marriages, pregnancies, alliances, mistakes, divorces, and healings.

Three babies are born between us. We have
not one disagreement ever; just laughter, travels,
altars, care, and lasting kindness. We call one
another *wife*, which really just means best friend.
Clothing is exchanged, trust freely offered.

Years in, my marriage ends, and then hers.
Several more moons go by, and she finds a new
guy who manages to frighten all of her friends.
I'm suspicious from moment one, and so are
those who love her. Over time, her voice changes,
becoming somehow haunted. Her friends see it
clearly; the word *grifter* materializes, shape-shifter
of the worst kind, to describe this guy. Texts go
unanswered; she slips away.

I'll learn later he's controlling her phone. The
brief contact I do have with her is as if with a
veritable stranger. Each time we speak, she sounds
less herself, more condescending. It's impossible
to comprehend, but a couple of friends keep the
faith with me. While we pull away, hoping that
somehow, some way she'll escape his clutches
and come back to us, we are afraid, but trusting.
Forcing her to cut off communication with her
strongest support system—her friends and her

children—real darkness descends. We have no clue when this will end.

Two years in, I receive a call—she's uncontrollably weeping. The abuse, the terror is finally shared. The stories I assumed I'd made up are all true, heartbreaking. She's speaking in her own voice again. She's been called the most inexcusable names; I make the mistake of listening to some of the recordings she made when he relegated her to the back seat of the car and shouted epithets at her. She's on the phone with me as she drives north to her family, ten hours over two days, explaining how it all unfolded. She begins reclaiming her dignity, her family, her heart. She changes all of her passwords, and I'm sure she's returning to us.

And yet, within five more days she calls again, her voice repossessed. She's going back to him. The hardest move I'll ever make in the arc of our twenty-year friendship is telling her to cease contact with me that day, until she's really ready to leave him. I wanted that boundary to feel good, but it never did.

Sometimes the finest offer we can make is a boundary. This one sent a clear message to her spirit.

Staring into the sky over the ensuing year, I pray for mercy for her: may she escape him and begin yet again. A year passes; my phone rings. "May I come," she asks, "to make amends?" In *her* voice.

We meet in a hotel bar, both of us shaking. She looks exhausted, beaten down. I take her hand; she's really back.

The delicate dance of letting myself love her again and risking more pain begins. I stay close to myself, offering her the best of what I've learned since, only when she asks. A quality of softness reveals itself; the boundary I've installed gives way to the tender homecoming of our decades of friendship.

Slowly she comes into clearer focus; the awful names she was called are peeled off, the holes in her energy field patched up by the love she receives from all of her closest friends. She yields to our prayers, her face transforms. I even find myself softening in her presence, finding respect for the years of painful choices she'd made. After a time, we don't need to speak of any of it.

Throughout the time of separation from her, all I could do was pray. Artist and writer Anne Truitt wrote, "Our deepest intimacy is that which trues us on a spiritual plumb line with the force from which we came and to which we go."[4]

Despite the chasm of time, the fresh intimacy we find is the energy that has held us on this plumb line. An unmistakable openness blossoms in both of us, continuing months later, discovering that we never lost our connection. All those prayers have been answered, and my wife is back.

In those years of losing one of my closest friends, prayer coursed through my being, in the form of words, wishes, asking . . . Prayers help us make sense of the difficult, especially in the face of unfamiliar challenge, lulling us into more emotional resourcefulness.

May your prayers soften you in the face of grief, moving you to hold both joy and sadness simultaneously. May you swiftly locate the words and attitudes to usher yourself into your realms of healing.

What is your prayer today?

Please write it, then whisper it, then speak it aloud.

Can you feel how your prayer lends stability to your being?

Is there any person or circumstance in which you know a simple prayer might be the only way in which you can serve? What does that prayer sound like?

Is there any boundary you might need to put in place in order to set yourself free?

THE ALTAR OF YOUR HEART

Have you ever been inspired by a devotional space in someone's home or a shop, whereupon seeing it, you suddenly want to do a clearing of your stuff and make your surroundings more intentional? There are physical altars that evoke within us a sense of the ineffable, the mystical, and there is also the altar within the heart. Perhaps right before we fall asleep, that's where we might find ourselves bowing with reverence, tending to ourselves naturally.

By some grace, early in my spiritual formation I'm welcomed into a small group of three women a few years older than me, all of whom shine in their respective fields: a world-renowned makeup artist, a stylist who rose up with some of the most influentially artful photographers of our time, and a supermodel with the humble heart of a bodhisattva. Each is an exemplar of appreciation, compassion, and wisdom. I won't know for decades how much their kindnesses toward me will impact my work, parenting, homemaking, art, writing—everything.

Their devotional spaces are replete with prayerful, intimate objects honoring their teachers and studies. Antique textiles, framed images, statues, talismans, stones . . . each item is a sacred conversation with an era I'll never fully know. Sensing a certain maturity unfolding as I spend more time in their homes, I feel invited toward more meditation, practice, and silence.

Decades pass, during which I find myself creating purposeful energetic altars in my own spaces. Each time we move, I create them anew, even on my travels, on desks in tiny hotel rooms. No matter how diminutive, each altar seems to generate a quality of stability and order within my family and heart, a foundational place to land, to start again. There are arrangements of objects, and then there are *altars*. I define an altar as a location for deep care, gratitude, safety, and remembrance.

Experiencing the sacred spaces of others continues to transform the way I care for my own home, reminding me to stop, rest, and listen. Waking in the mornings and making offerings of water, food and tea, as I light a candle and a stick of incense, I am opening, softening.

My dear colleague and friend Tracee Stanley's book *Radiant Rest* is a key resource in my personal practice and professional teaching. Her resonant offerings on the spiritual importance of deep rest and restoration have shifted the way I use my voice, words, and energy to serve and transmit.

Years ago she gifted me a letterpress piece on which is printed her poem "Householder's Prayer." This prayer moves me to revere the most quotidian moments and locate the altar in my own heart.

For forty days, practicing Tracee's "Altar of the Heart"[5] nidra, I learn to navigate my consciousness toward the innermost altar and rest there. Creating a relationship to my innermost self, I find a simple connection inward, right on time, long overdue. With Tracee's permission, I am honored to share her prayer with you.

Householder's Prayer

The altar is in my heart.

The sun and moon are my gurus. I trust the earth to support me.

Each time I close my eyes, I enter the void. My heart is the portal to my sacred cave.

I notice the flow of my beloveds' breath
as they fall asleep, and I synchronize my
breath to the flow of love.

I place a blessing in the pause between the
breaths.

I hold the power to create a new reality with
every thought. I honor silence as a blessing.

I explore who I am and who I am not in the
mirror of relationship.
I question my beliefs with curiosity and
courage.

I honor my ancestors.

I lay down all self-doubt with compassion
and forgiveness. I remember the light of my
soul as I enter the dream state.

I recall the beauty of truth as I transition
from sleep to waking. I know the vibration
of truth.

I remember that nothing is mundane.

I honor the power of the transition as a portal to transformation. Everything is an offering. My life is a sacred ritual.[6]

I place all self-doubt, self-judgment, and fear at the altar of my heart to be transformed, along with my trust, light, and clarity to be amplified.

May we all continue our trajectory of healing.

Might you have a space in your home that you can clear to create an altar of your own?

Might you have a prayer to offer yourself toward your own healing?

What are you placing at the altar of your heart today or in this time of your life?

Can you tenderly appreciate the simple sacredness of your smallest acts of householding?

YOUR STABLE INNER ATMOSPHERE

When I was invited to offer practice and presence to the clinicians on the pediatric oncology unit at NewYork-Presbyterian Hospital in New York City, I felt an unwavering pull to say yes. Traveling uptown with my son, who was about eight or nine years of age at the time, we offered our presence to the doctors, nurses, children, and families, experiencing moments of healing neither of us will ever forget.

From Fulton Street to 42nd Street, then 42nd to 110th, my son and I travel the length of Manhattan. Tired at the end of a long city day of school and teaching classes, we lean on one another for both train rides, fortifying ourselves for our fourth visit to the pediatric ward, offering simple presence for the kids and parents on the oncology floor.

On previous visits, we've offered meditation to the nurses and doctors in the break room and Reiki to the kids and parents who've been here for too long, so early in their lives. Today, we meet

two forlorn, exhausted parents with their three-year-old girl, an angelic child with copious blond curls, as she is about to come off the respirator to see if she can breathe on her own. Her situation is critical.

Quietly, I offer Reiki to her mom, who does her best to receive. For her this is a new feeling. I can sense the years of her adrenalized state as tears stream down her face in rivulets. As I rest my hands on her sloping shoulders, her head straining to stay aloft on her spine, I do my best not to cry. My son places his gentlest hands on the feet of her tiny daughter as she sleeps, his offering of care to her healing body. We stay for several minutes before visiting with a few other patients.

The train ride home is usually a slew of questions, but today my son and I share silence. Feelings of grief, guilt, and gratitude commingle within me, and all I can do is give myself empathy, soften and steady myself inwardly, and remind myself of my humanity. I'll learn in years to come that these moments of self-stewardship are a crucial step in learning to stabilize myself in the traumatic situations in which I'm serving.

As we lean on one another on our way home, I know that this regular contact with my boy will someday come to an end, and I realize how lucky I am that we're healthy, connected, and literally holding each other up on this train.

That boy is ten years older now, on his own. And when things are especially challenging, I like to think some trace of these visits lives in him when he comes across challenges. Personally, I find myself repeatedly placing a hand on my heart, turning my attention around, slowing myself almost to a halt, and repeating these words: *How human of me to feel anxious in this moment, fearful, lost. How human of me to ache for answers, insights, healings that will never come. How human of me to not have any solutions to this pain and unfairness.*

These are the moments when cultivating and maintaining our stable inner atmosphere is everything.

When do you most need inward stability, and how do you offer it to yourself?

How does having empathy for yourself take shape? Words, practices, solitude . . .?

Do you have any inclination toward volunteering at this time in your life? Have you any notion of what that might look like?

How does your practice of offering yourself empathy translate to a more stable inner atmosphere?

OFFERINGS OF STEADINESS

Our presence is the primary offering we can make in most situations. As I venture into hours of service, writing and studying as a chaplaincy candidate, the experiences I'm having in local communities are priceless. Mostly, all I can offer is presence, steadiness.

> During the tenuous end-of-pandemic months when nobody knows exactly what's what, we're still masking up. At a local shelter, a few of us from the Upaya Street Ministry are about to serve salad, soup, and dessert to about fifty souls. It's my first time, and I'm nervous.
>
> Once everything is laid out in the industrial kitchen at the back of the main room of the shelter, an assembly line materializes, with volunteers and shelter workers cobbling together piles of to-go boxes, everything neatly arranged on carts. Two of us are assigned to wheel the carts toward the entrance door, where we stand sentry at this portal to folks who've not eaten all day, likely longer.

As we begin handing out boxes, a sense of purpose drops anchor within us. Some of the clients offer swift, silent nods, others are all smiles and say, "Thank you so much" and "Maybe I can come back again for more?" I say, "I'm not sure, but I'll ask." About ten minutes pass.

The smell of cigarettes wafts through the door. I presume this marks the end of the meal here, but another small line forms. If there's food left, I'm told, feel free to offer seconds. I peek around to the makeshift patio, really a covered section of the parking lot, to see the folks I've just met now eating at picnic tables, conversing over the homemade brownies baked by the broader practice community. Some folks return for seconds, maybe this is their only substantial meal for the next several days. I'm beginning to comprehend the stark, daunting reality of what it means to suffer from food insecurity.

Noticing myself toggling between focused attention and open presence, my earlier nervousness fades away as day turns to evening. Something changes within me; taking several conscious breaths, I feel myself stabilizing. A steadiness emerges from deep inside, an intuition that I belong here, serving seconds to these kind humans who've suffered circumstances any one of us might face. I stay very still, thankful, overtaken by a sense of grace.

Moving beyond what's comfortable into the unknown, volunteering is part of my personal process of formation as I learn to care and serve amidst uncertainty. Sharing a glimpse of these moments is how I choose to share my own engagement with you as I aim to understand my future role of offering some steadiness where it's needed most.

Is there a community nearby where you might be able to offer time, energy, or resources?

Do you sense the presumption your mind makes that such an offering isn't plausible?

Are you willing to quietly bring your stability to someone with less security?

If this feels too daunting, is there someone with whom you work or live who might benefit from your simple offering of steadiness?

7

Safely Trusting
Your Wisdom

○

In the second grade, my classroom teacher Mrs. Petrilli instilled a generous experience of trust in myself, after a year of being belittled and diminished in my previous teacher's first-grade class. Leading with humor, Mrs. Petrilli transmitted a playful blend of possibility and humility that I've carried with me throughout my life. Her encouragement still reverberates.

When a colleague, teacher, parent, or friend offers us space to feel safe enough to trust ourselves, that inner trust yields a sense of both confidence and humility regarding our innate wisdom. With those grounded qualities, we're more able to be present amidst the fragility of our world. Feeling safe leads to clearer access to your intuition.

Trusting in yourself allows you to offer and receive genuine care in your interactions. That trust becomes a demonstrable quality of restfulness in your system that can be felt by others with whom you're in relationship.

Do you know someone who carries this trust in themselves? How do you feel around them? Their inner trust is transmitted in how they show up, and the impact of their clarity resonates. Throughout this chapter, you'll get in touch with your own inner coherence, arriving at and refining a sense of trust within yourself.

DISSOLVING DOUBT

I bow to the teachers of my childhood and young adulthood who reinforced my inward connection, their gift of trust slowly becoming my own as the years unfold, providing impressions of warmth, care, levity, and consistency.

At around age fourteen, during my first year of high school, I'm walking the halls, wondering, *Is* this *subject my passion? Are* you *the teacher who's going to make this life make sense to me?* The students congregating at the brown lockers all seem so happy, established, and at ease in their bodies. I have no idea who I am or what will come of this education. And I feel alone for the early part of the year.

Then art class begins, with a long, loud, "Welcome in!" from Mrs. Hochberg. A flourish of red hair and a brightly colored apron gives me an inexplicable feeling of belonging. Art is *everywhere* in this room, from paintings to gallery posters; I feel as though I'm in a foreign land here and yet completely at home. Within minutes, Mrs.

Hochberg delivers a promise that we'll be visiting museums in New York City this year. Something settles within me—a feeling that I'm in the right place. I'm safe here.

Setting about learning as much as I can, I spend time during my free periods sitting in on Mrs. Hochberg's other classes. Taking extra time with her artist friends who visit her classroom, I absorb their brushstrokes, mannerisms, words, color choices, and practices. A trust in my capacity emerges. I begin believing in myself, in my artistry, in my place in the world.

One or two of my first pieces from that year still exist at my Dad's house, tender watercolor and gouache images of women's faces, wrapped in scarves, textiles, and saturated hues. Painting those faces gave me an intimacy with femininity, texture, proportion, and color, understandings still blossoming in my art practices as I grow older.

In the years to follow, art will be a saving grace for me, a thread wending its way through my emotional and physical healing. Daily miniature watercolor paintings will mark days one through forty as I begin my life free from marijuana and alcohol in my forties. Small cards painted and written on handmade paper become earnest ways to offer thankfulness as well as apologies. Eventually, in my early fifties, a small local gallery offers to show my paintings in New Mexico—a full circle indeed. Art gives me ways to arrange my mind, my evolution, and my ongoing internal inquiries.

Doubt is a topic about which I'm asked often. In every realm of our visual media landscape, we are led to see ourselves as lacking or in need; from advertising to social media, we're taught that we're not enough. The practice of meditation is a crucial puzzle piece in managing my doubtful tendencies. Sitting offers a small window of internal intimacy in which I can apprehend the earliest traces of doubt before they become an intractable inner dialogue. Practiced with consistency, meditation seems to melt doubt away.

As the years of sitting unfold, I can name a handful of moments in which I've forgotten myself for minutes at a time. In Zen, that's known as "no-trace." Moments in which I can see beneath the persona I've created to reality *as it is*, past the doubts of the little girl within, to the wise older woman who pays no mind to any of it.

When I sit, I can easily see the narratives within that seem to shut down my heart. If I can stay still long enough, sitting opens a glimpse into what *else* is true, where there is no need, just a bow of respectful presence, and then I can do whatever is next, be it the laundry or making dinner. Hours and years of practice help me see that doubt is an imaginal fabrication that keeps me from myself, from my art, from silence. And finishing any project—whether it's painting a watercolor, writing this book, or sending my son to college—requires that I dissolve the part of me that doubts so the real story of possibility and hope can emerge.

The voice of truth, love, silence, tenderness, and nurturance—we all need this from deep within ourselves. Have you found this voice within you? When is that voice most available?

Has doubt gripped you in the past? Has doubt ever stopped you or changed your trajectory?

What practice helps you get familiar with your doubt so you can loosen the grip of it?

Can you name a teacher who's embraced your potential, leading you to trust in your own gifts?

CHILDHOOD SELF

Reaching back through time and across distances to connect with our childhood self, we get in touch with our most vulnerable, tenderly lived life. We hold our own tiny hands, reaching back in time to provide a feeling of care, of being seen. This is an evolving, generous practice—one I deeply value and prioritize—that offers perspective and peace.

Above my standing desk where I'm writing right now sits a small walnut tray with a few items: a miniature vase made by a local Diné artist, a small piece of clear fluorite on which sits a tiny bronze Buddha, the Empowerment card from the *Daily Ceremony Deck*, and a picture of me at seven years old. I'm wearing gold-framed aviator glasses, pigtails, a plaid button-down shirt, and little bell-bottomed jeans, which are rolled up to reveal striped socks on my feet, and with all my might, I'm hugging the base of a palm tree.

Taken in Hallandale, Florida, on Hollywood Beach near where my grandparents lived, this photograph brings me back to the haven of my grandparents' home and their love. I felt seen and deeply appreciated then, especially by my grandma, who was my biggest fan. When I look at this image, I see her standing nearby in my mind, feeling the warmth of her attention, her hand holding mine. She's not in the image, but she's there next to my dad, who captured the picture. Gramma Belle.

Her love informs how I love my son now: unconditionally, steadily, truly. Offering the quality of grandmother's heart even though I'm still in my fifties and the mother of a teenager, what I'm learning from staring at this tiny altar every day is to reach back in time to love that child, and to see everything through the kindness in *her* heart.

Somehow this miniature altar to my childhood self teaches me through time, offering new information and intelligence from someone long gone. If the spirit of *bodhicitta*, an awakened heart of service, is a willingness to not know, to bear witness, and to take compassionate action with full effort and imperfect results, this miniscule altar somehow connects me to the essence of this heart.

In a journal, on a shelf, or even on these pages, you're invited to create an altar to your childhood self.

If you don't have access to photographs, this can be a letter to your childhood self at a certain age. If you have some photos, arrange them with some precious items or words where you'll see them often.

Listen for the teachings that might be transmitted through these many years, via the voices of those who'd still love to be of some use to you now.

As Gramma Belle did for me, how might you love any human, child, partner, colleague, or friend just as they are, without needing for them to be different?

SENSING SAFETY

Let's speak of the ones in our lives who've helped us feel safe, seen, trusted, and trusting. Below, I honor the ones who've helped me feel safe, and as you read, you're invited to remember your earliest and best, along with your most recent and supportive friends.

At the end of our shared blocks, connecting two neighborhoods, stood two parallel, shoulder-height fences with dirt between them, the only place where neither of our mothers could see us. We call it the golden gate, even though it's chain link. This was before devices and cell phones, so my best friend Karen and I call one another on rotary phones from our homes and plan to meet there for missions of all sorts, especially if one of our parents is shouting and cross. We meet, sit, talk, and roller-skate in the street together. We reassure one another that all will be well. We laugh and dream and wonder about this or that boy, and our futures.

As we get older, we smoke cigarettes there, seated in the dirt, knees tucked to our chests, crossing our fingers in hope that our moms or someone else's parents won't show up and see us. Somehow our time at the end of the block goes forever uninterrupted. Karen remains a dear, heart friend, in deep service to children and families as chief of pediatric palliative care in a prominent cancer hospital, and we're still in contact.

Then in the seventh grade, it's Katie. We spend hours drawing, cutting out magazine images, passing notes in class, giving ourselves new names (Victoria and Ashley—so much cooler), and discussing boys we like. Sprawled out on her flowered bedspread, laughing, listening to the Police's *Synchronicity* album again, then Duran Duran, we're inseparable; nothing can touch us as we grow into being best friends. Still in touch, we're both now sober; she's creating as ever and always just one text message away.

Throughout my childhood, during summers in upstate New York, years of sleepaway camp deliver a sense of safety for which I will never stop being grateful. Finding ourselves in a small bunk together, about ten girls, summer after summer with a few additions and subtractions.

A day is a month, and our daily learnings help us become who we are. Forging and sometimes forsaking connections to our bodies, to our mentors and counselors, to each other, this is where it all happens: first kisses, first instances of body dysmorphia, faking being sick to get out of swim instruction, sheer elation at all-camp games, hints of eating disorders . . . We scream at the top of our lungs during sports and hold hands as we walk, singing, swaying, weeping as each summer suddenly comes to a halt, and we go back to our own towns, thankful for the feelings of belonging to that place, to each other.

There are myriad generous colleagues early in my yoga training and dear friends and mentors past and present who take me under their wings. More recently, there is the sangha at the Upaya Zen Center with whom I've shared the quietest, most transformative moments of my spiritual upbringing.

My closest friends, from my thirties through my fifties, are the ones whom I've chosen carefully, the ones who've chosen me, for whom I've written poems and with whom I've carved out travel and space to celebrate and mourn together.

Fewer in number as the years go on, they know precisely who they are and how our relationship is continuously evolving toward more care and nurturance.

As I consider each face in remembrance, I realize that every setting and soul mentioned has moved me to take refuge in *myself*. Thank you to those humans for their subtractive care that's left ample space for my sense of safety to unfold.

A sense of sanctuary is felt when a person or setting offers their spacious presence in which you're inspired to trust in yourself, to turn inward and deeply reflect, to take refuge in your own silence. Taking refuge is an act of handing over my heart to, or finding comfort in, a teaching or a concept that holds truth or meaning for me. In certain aspects of my studies, I take refuge in that which silences the mind, expands a feeling of safety, and softens the heart, often instantaneously and usually wordlessly.

> *The sutras only say to take refuge in the buddha of yourself. They don't say to take refuge in some other buddha. If you don't take refuge in your own nature, there is no other place of refuge.*
> —RED PINE, *The Platform Sutra*

What does this practice of taking refuge mean to you?

Is there any teaching in which you've taken refuge in the past?

Did that quiet your mind, offer some sense of safety, or open your heart to a new understanding?

Here are a few possible practices:

- Taking a walk on a familiar path
- Listening to three consecutive breaths
- Sitting quietly for ten or twenty minutes
- Standing in front of a piece of art, or an altar, that holds meaning for you

And when you practice taking refuge, can you feel your constructs and assumptions about yourself beginning to disappear?

Who helps you feel truly safe to be yourself in these times? Is it a teacher, a colleague, a friend?

Might you offer them some words or art to reflect your thankfulness?

PRACTICE AS REALIZATION

Questioning and wondering if I'd ever be a capable enough mother, my hope from the start was just to be an example of security and spaciousness. The glimpses of trust in myself come rarely, quietly at first. I try to observe as dispassionately as I can, both on my meditation cushion and in daily moments with my kid. It seems as though the more I practice, the more connected I feel to silence, the more I can trust myself to offer the most appropriate response in my parenting.

Real awakening is just like anything else—
a whisper, a slight tilt of a hand, a wink of the eye;
it is almost silent and doesn't need attention.
—SALLIE TISDALE, *Women of the Way*

He sits with me at our dining room table for a few minutes this afternoon, spring sky cloudless, wind howling. Seventeen years in, my son's just begun speaking about a moment of reckoning amongst his friends. Things I wish he didn't have to manage yet.

Whatever the full story is, it's clearly hard for him to share; we've already been sitting here for some time. I know my work here is to offer supportive silence, to stay with softness, to just be present. Lately I've been consciously cultivating valences of patience within my system for both of us.

He's in a moral quandary, and it's apparent from his tale that choices are being made in the direction of the right thing. I say as little as I can.

We sit silently for a while. He's fidgeting with his fingers, trying to find the words, rolling the matter around internally. I can take credit for *not* talking, not asking too many questions. Somehow my own meditation practice, befriending doubt and making my way back to my breathing, is right here, helping me feel more at ease being unable to solve anything. I remind myself to breathe. I let it all be.

He finally begins to speak a bit, trusting me. The silence eases us into an earnest connection, the soft part of my fierce grandmother's heart beating patiently. Still listening, in the safety and trust of this grounded silence, I'm finally able to offer a handful of brief, thoughtful words that might serve here. A quick hug marks the end of this exchange; we're both thankful.

Real transformation is grounded in an experience of connection and radical intimacy with the world. It is about the realization that awakening is not an individual experience. It is liberation in our intimate relatedness with and through all beings. Awakening, then, is ultimately social.
—ROSHI JOAN HALIFAX,
"Practice for a World at Risk," *Lion's Roar*

Awakening is our practice, and realization continuously opens—in my heart, yours, and in the hearts of those around us. The realization you have in any moment creates a ripple of consciousness emanating throughout space and time. We're not separate from anything, anyone, anywhere, even when it might *seem* that we are.

When I sit in meditation, you benefit. When you sit, I benefit. At the dining room table, when I manage to sit supportively still, my son feels heard and safe enough to solve his own quandaries. Meditation practice provides a structure that nourishes our experience of intimacy within ourselves, which yields a feeling of safety and inward peace for all.

What I've come to understand is that there isn't actually a *destination*, whether in practice or a conversation. Realization is already present, answers are already unfolding. In Zen, sitting quietly and observing the breath is both practice and realization. As are lighting incense, copying verses, cleaning intentionally, and bowing deeply.

Sitting still so my son can safely sort through difficulty is both practice and realization.

Practice, realization. In this quiet moment, they're one and the same. Maybe I've been practicing just to have trust while sitting in uncomfortable silences, without trying to help or fix. And when I manage to muddle through a vexing interaction with trust for myself, I'm realization in practice, serving others along with me.

The lengthier meditation periods inform moments like this; when several minutes go by with no recognizable feeling of safety or peace within my body, sometimes I can be quiet enough internally so another quality of listening can arise. The moment at the dining room table with my son is evidence that these humble efforts toward inner and outer peace aren't mine alone.

Can you think of an example when someone's listened well, safely inviting you to come to your own solution or conclusion?

Do you have any practices that also feel like realization (meaning, when you engage with them, you catch glimpses of the simplicity at the heart of everything)?

With whom can you practice letting go of solutions and just listening?

Next time you take your seat in meditation—or right this moment as you're reading—arrange your posture to reflect this truth: *I am practicing realization, and I am realization, practicing.*

RELATING TO THE PRESENT

Quotidian tasks offer freedom from my past and persona, inviting me to reconnect to the present. Releasing the need to do everything just right, sinking into the work at hand, I practice letting go of habitual thoughts, cultivating a non-mediated relationship to the present moment.

During months in residence at the Upaya Zen Center, we're engaging in a silent work practice known as *samu*. During my initial visit, I'm assigned to the housekeeping team. We begin with an opening circle that feels welcoming. I'm learning in these weeks what it means to let go of my agenda, to listen, to care for spaces as well as we'd care for humans. Each day is a new chance to dive in to the act of tidying silently, with an attitude of patience, freed from the artifice of the personality.

Walking to my assigned building, cleaning gloves on and bucket in hand, my mind is empty. Washing sinks and surfaces, sweeping floors and scrubbing toilets feels freeing. I realize that nothing needs to be perfect, but when I commit myself to it, the work is done well and with ease. In the silence of those morning cleanings, I'm more relaxed than I've felt in years.

Whether with your feet on the ground or a seat on the cushion, cleaning or creating, returning to this present moment is a *practice*. With practice, I become less attached to outcome, less connected to habits of thinking, less obsessed with goals, and more curious about the process. When I don't know how to do or find something, I ask for help without feeling pressure, attending to the work without losing myself. There's a pulsation I can sense, toggling between two types of attention.

On one hand, I can focus, drop into my body, and be deeply present for what I need to do, whether I'm sitting with a dying person, folding towels, or cleaning bathrooms. At the same time, another quality of attention is there—a quality of attention that is reflective, panoramic, inclusive, unperturbed, and nonjudgmental. In certain moments, I feel like I can clearly see what's needed.

In a nonmediated, emergent relationship with the present, I'm more able to see through habitual thoughts or the outward behaviors of others to the struggle or grief that might be present. Catching a tone from my partner, I can practice curiosity and realize he's nervous about a meeting, instead of taking his unease personally. And I can detect traces of intolerance within myself in those instances, realizing there's some attitude I can release. In this practice of letting go of thoughts I've unconsciously held for so long and instead relating to the present, something shifts.

If I fully immerse myself in what I'm doing, dropping haste and perfection to engage with the present more completely, I'm more able to relate to the moment just as it is. Most days since, I feel an available inner tenderness.

In what task(s) are you able to let go of the mind and relate to the present?

When can you observe yourself veering into haste, past or future?

With whom do you find it easy to relate to in the present?

When you attune to what is present in this moment, can you see that what you're experiencing now is precisely what's needed?

8
Actualizing
Acceptance

Like many of us, I've struggled with self-acceptance throughout my life. Exhausting myself by turning my attention outward, prioritizing external validation, I've watched myself deny my truth by staying in relationships longer than appropriate, numbing myself with substances, and overworking to hide from what I'm feeling. In this time of my life, a practice of actualizing acceptance brings a sense of peace.

WHO I'M BECOMING

Each movement toward actualizing acceptance—both for what's happening within me and around me—yields initial resistance that leads eventually to a mercifully quiet inner landscape. Oftentimes I've no idea how to proceed, but I place a hand on my heart to remind myself that I'm doing okay, to keep going, to trust in not knowing. The instinctive ego pushes back and resists uncertainty until this kindness toward myself reveals the terrain of freedom.

Sitting across the table from my son in a remote café in Kyoto, he and I are talking closely. Along with apologies for years of small thinking and misplaced priorities as his mom, I make it clear that I'm aware of my missteps in his early life and share about what I would do differently if I had a second chance. We feel into the possibilities and move into a new realm of respect; instead of being hard on myself for these chapters of my parenting, I'm thankful for his willingness to listen. We're in this together; our mutual offering of groundedness grants us both a sense of acceptance.

○

Standing at the kitchen island as my partner
chops veggies for a salad, his pale blue eyes
focused intently as he moves the mandoline
to create paper-thin carrot slices, his earnest
transmission of care. I feel us both aging,
suddenly sensing an upwelling of love for the
grace we're bringing to one another, ten years in.
Even in times of misunderstanding, this kindness
anchors us, reminding us to stay the course. Our
steady mutual acceptance is all of it.

○

On a blustering cold winter day in the Southwest,
two close friends and I are tending a substantial
fire in the woodburning stove as I ceremoniously
liberate myself from one of the strangest seasons
of my life, releasing self-judgment and doubt
into the fire. I'm making a conscious attempt at
acceptance again. Standing with me through
decades of relationships, moves, and professional
iterations, these two true friends offer pure,

steadfast ballast for my process of evolution. Even when they disagree with my choices, they offer presence, support, and acceptance, consistently reminding me to stay close to myself.

Although just blips in the arc of my life's trajectory, in each of these scenes, there's been a palpable shift from doubt to willingness. These spacious moments of softening point to practices of actualizing acceptance.

As you read on, take three grounding breaths, allowing your attention to rest lightly on the physical experience of breathing, deep in the body. Inspired by Roshi Joan Halifax as she teaches meditation during G.R.A.C.E. trainings at Upaya, this practice is a way to practice actualizing acceptance.

As you inhale, gather your attention and care from outside of yourself to deep *within*.

With each exhalation, grow your spine taller, and let your attention *settle* in your body.

When you sense your mind producing thoughts in the field of your consciousness, gently and firmly bring yourself back to the sound and the sensation of the breath each time you notice it happening. And if for any reason the breath doesn't feel safe, attune to the sounds around you as anchors for your awareness.

Continue practicing gathering your attention by letting it rest lightly on the physical sensation of your inhale. Then exhale, letting your attention rest within you.

Notice your posture. How you're sitting influences the quality of mind you're cultivating. Practicing a quality of uprightness, of dignity, your capacity to uphold yourself in any situation is enhanced.

Cultivate a strong yet flexible back; strong, supportive, and present.

Sense your front body soft and open, breath moving deeply into the body. Sense the stability at the core of your being.

Strong back, soft front. Equanimity and compassion.

Instead of our habitual strong, guarded front and soft, defended back, we cultivate a strong back with a soft front, inviting us to be fully present to the world, to each other, and to reality.

FLOWERS ARE SANCTUARIES

The relationship I have with flowers dates to my childhood, when my mom would drop me off at her sister's house, and together my aunt and I would create arrangements for her small flower delivery business. My aunt respected me as a human and valued my assistance. The time with her was special, the artist in me felt seen, and since then, my time in Nature offers a haven for me, and each flower is a tiny, pristine sanctuary. Where do you feel that feeling of refuge? Where are the smallest sanctuaries in your world?

For the first time in ages, I'm home by myself for several days. Seated silently at the far end of the dining room table staring at snow falling, I can see the trees receiving dense concentrations of snowflakes. The forest seems to be breathing. My son's away, my partner is traveling for work—the quiet is both deafening and a balm for my entire being.

Having folded all the remaining laundry and tidied the house, the afternoon mercifully lingers. While arranging some books to scaffold today's

writing session, I recall that I've got fresh lacy-edged tulips on the kitchen counter, fleeting and precious, like little women. I start trimming their stems at a slow cadence, taking thirty minutes or so, and staring into each of their faces. Each is a living being, a whole personality, telling me stories about life and death, care and consequences. Flowers are sanctuaries. I fall in love with each of them.

Placing them into three vases at three different altars around the house—the kitchen, my desk, and my bedroom—I realize it's twenty minutes past five in the evening, and meditation begins in ten minutes. Drawn to the cushion, I quietly sit. I try not to berate myself for postponing the writing.

Words and thoughts dance across my mind like light bulbs, lighting up, then going dark. It reminds me of catching a firefly in a jar at no more than eight years old and the smell of that summer evening. Staring at the trapped being feels upsetting to me. I remember letting her go immediately. *If only I knew how to do that with my thoughts*, I think. What floats in next is a fascicle by Dogen, the story of the udumbara blossom, which in this tale stands for all the precious teachings.

Dogen Zenji devoted an entire fascicle in his monumental body of work, the *Shobogenzo*, to praising a particular blossom, the *udumbara*, the flower of enlightenment, said to bloom once every three thousand years. In this tale, the Buddha's disciple Mahakasyapa, a patriarch of Chan (the Chinese precedent for Zen), receives the entire body of the teachings in one moment, as the Buddha holds up an udumbara flower to indicate the scope and the treasury of the teachings.

> *At the Assembly of a million beings on Vulture Peak,*
> *the World-Honored One held up an udumbara blossom and*
> *blinked. Then, Mahakasyapa smiled. The World-Honored One*
> *said, "I have the treasury of the true dharma eye, the wondrous*
> *heart of nirvana. I entrust it to Mahakasyapa."*
> —EIHEI DOGEN,
> *Treasury of the True Dharma Eye*

So many ways to turn this in my mind. By studying a flower, we are studying our own fleeting existence. Flowers are teachers, refuges, and reminders of life and death, coming and going. How can we live fully in the sanctuary of the present moment?

What is vital here is that you give expression to the flower of
your Self, the flower of here and now, and allow it to blossom as
completely and as naturally as it can in every moment of your life.
That flower of your Self, that flower of here and now, is your life!
—EIHEI DOGEN AND KOSHO UCHIYAMA ROSHI,
How to Cook Your Life

What's ending in your life these days?

What might be beginning?

Like holding up the flower, what are you holding up in
your life?

What might you offer your future self as a teaching on
impermanence, from the vantage point of today?

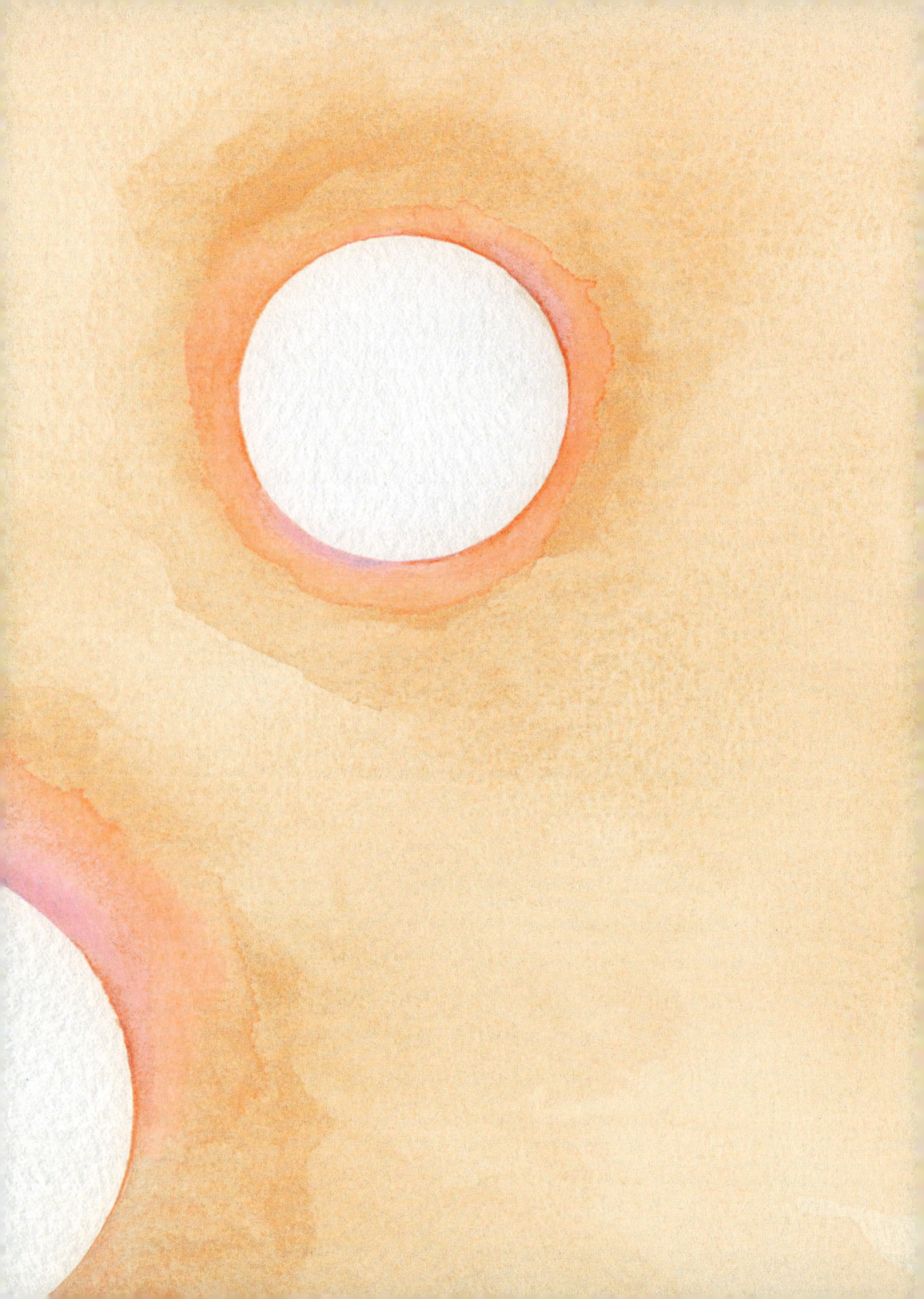

THE PRESENT MOMENT

Continuously returning to the present moment has been my primary practice for the past few humbling years. Sitting very still, hiking up thousands of feet, writing, cooking, sitting with a dying patient, or cleaning the sink, the present moment is waiting for us to rest, to take refuge, and to cease all the thinking.

Snow falling, wind whipping through the valley as dark settles in. We've been sitting for several hours. Dainin, a dear friend since my days in New York City, is both a Zen priest and an MD, currently serving as *shuso*, or head student, for this winter practice period. We're engaged in a ceremony to affirm her role, and when it's my turn to ask a question of our head student, I freeze. All I can think to ask her is, "What *is* this?"

Sitting across the meditation hall from one another, we lock eyes, several years seem to fold into this one moment of time. She responds only with tears, silence. I thank her. She continues, customarily, "May your life go well."

Entering the stream of the Soto Zen teachings back in 2020, at the height of the pandemic, the Upaya Zen Center was closed to visitors, even the locals. I participated and practiced diligently in my own space virtually, even though I was just one mile away.

The ways in which Roshi Joan kept highlighting the resilience required to keep opening even when we feel like closing, giving up, and turning away became a balm for me. "Stay the course," she'd say over and over; her medicine of steadiness. *How serious her commitment is*, I would think to myself. Each time I'm with her, an important aspect of her transmission is endurance.

But opening to the softness within the rigor has become my practice. Finding both the tenderness and the strength in my own heart is a gift I continue to unwrap. Consciously allowing my heart to break open and lighten each time I listen to the dharma, the teachings, I'm learning to let go of everything I hold too tightly—my confusion, my personality, ideas about the future, achievements, a lifetime of ignorance . . . Learning that I cannot define myself, and awakening is continuous. There's nothing to hold on to.

As time goes on, I'm opening more deeply to the chants, the gestures, and the koans, or "family stories." And within these apertures of inquiry, I find myself disappearing and dissolving, releasing all the strata of my identity.

The Heart Sutra's final syllables become a beacon for my practice and my occupied mind: *Gate Gate Paragate Parasamgate Bodhi Svaha*, or "Gone, gone. Gone beyond. Wisdom beyond wisdom."

From the translation in the Upaya Zen Center liturgy reader, "This mantra is luminous, unequalled and supreme. It relieves all suffering. It is genuine, not illusory."

No matter when you're reading this, your present moment might include challenges or possibly pain. Practice being attentive to illuminate the relevant lessons, and be willing to shed the rest. That process of shedding is how we release layers of identity and return to the gift of the present.

When pain is present, can you open your heart to what might be instructive about this moment?

When do you feel yourself disappearing into the moment, with no persona, no agenda, just full presence?

In what situation might it behoove you to practice letting go?

THE FULLNESS
OF EMPTINESS

Looking back at my early adulthood, revisiting moments during which I thought I knew it all, I feel empathy for those younger versions of myself, for the various ways in which I was filling spaces, being busy, garnering attention, succumbing to addiction. I can see how afraid I was of emptiness, quiet, and solitude. Realizing the fullness in emptiness now, I appreciate the fear I felt when I was younger and the burgeoning fearlessness I can sometimes feel now that I have a consistent practice.

We are sitting next to one another in the top row of a newly built stadium-seating auditorium classroom with priceless energy ricocheting between us. It's our senior year at Cornell, and we're taking a class on business etiquette, one of the most pertinent, useful classes I'll ever take.

We begin leaning into one another over weeks, literally and figuratively. We pass notes and begin quietly dating. He grew up in New York City,

which, compared to my Long Island, is downright exotic, exciting. He's got style; he's comfortable in his skin, which is everything. Plans are made on push-button wall phones—we won't have mobile phones for another five years—and pickups for college sleepovers happen in snowstorms.

After graduation, we decide we'll stay at his apartment in New York City with his mom, who remains a dear friend to me. She lets me work at her flower shop, which becomes the perfect counterpoint to my day job designing textiles on the twenty-first floor of an office building between Fifty-Fourth and Fifty-Fifth Streets, just off Sixth Avenue. Known for her elaborate, enormous arrays of flowers, she teaches me how to arrange extravagant beribboned bouquets of dozens of roses as I spend hours in her shop among still-life assemblages of ancient statues, columns, and mirrors. Time stops here, under her tutelage, and my appreciation for beauty begins in earnest.

In our early twenties, with the full support of our families, we move into a studio apartment in Gramercy, bringing with us a few antique pieces to create a tiny home of our dreams. The fact that the details of our first apartment together would someday be forgotten never enters our minds. We're full-blown adults, or so we think. Looking back at photos now, all I see is the fullness of youth and freedom in our faces. Together we make it through his years of law school, waiting tables, a prized internship, his first job at the best firm . . . Sofie the dog comes into our life, and we love each other more than we can imagine. But we're young, impressionable, and our interests diverge sooner than we could've fathomed.

When it's time to part ways, he generously helps me with my security deposit on an apartment just across the street so we can both take care of Sofie, our shared dogchild. Those early months feel lonely and empty compared to the perfect almost-family that had come to an end.

But this is where I begin figuring out how to be my own best friend.

My new place is a tiny alcove studio, with two tall, thin windows. Here I experiment with love and substances, and become a business owner. During the spring months, little white cherry blossoms appear on the trees just outside the second-floor windows, where I smoke and dream. I begin learning what taking care of myself means.

The emptiness becomes the source of my first attempts at writing, and I won't realize the value of this time and the poetry that arises until decades pass by. A close friend introduces me to my first yoga-teaching job. And then I meet a kind human who helps me exit the office life to open my studio, back in the days before yoga studios existed.

Emptiness is fullness; fullness is emptiness.

Riding unrelenting waves of uncertainty in our lives, letting go of what we *thought* needed to happen remains the practice, revealing fresh connection to ourselves, over and over again. When we feel most alone, we find ways to fill time, mining our own existence.

> *The richest part of life lies in the space*
> *between absence and presence.*
> —PICO IYER, *A Beginner's Guide to Japan*

As I look back on this time, I recall a meticulously arranged altar at which I almost never sat for meditation. Wanting desperately to engage in practice but just barely beginning, I was always bargaining with myself, resisting sitting instead of opening to the fullness of those seemingly empty moments, I had no tolerance for what felt like loneliness.

Today I feel compassion for the girl I was, who, in my mind's eye, keeps getting high and rearranging her color-coded books. I can feel her getting closer to herself but still caving in to various choices and cravings. Older now, more patient, my practice has become more of an invitation.

May the space between absence and presence teach us about the relationship between fullness and emptiness. May we see that emptiness is actually fullness, and savor what changes.

Are there any practices or humans offering you emptiness as fullness in this season?

Have you encountered any uncomfortable instances of emptiness in your life?

Where did that discomfort lead? Did you expect that outcome?

Can you see with some distance or passing of time the blessing of that emptiness?

LETTING GO, SETTLING IN

Still dark, today's faint pink winks at the inky-blue mountains as I fumble to my cushion again. Trying to be quiet for my partner who's still asleep, I light a stick of incense as quietly as I can. Holding the incense up near my forehead like my teachers do, I silently take refuge, recommit to my vows, place the stick in its holder, and stand. Bowing to my cushion, then to James (now seated upright in the bed), I turn to take my seat.

Clumsily arranging my body with some semblance of dignity, my next inhale lifts my sides, my exhale settles me. Allowing my breath to reach way down deep into my belly, thoughts arise and dissolve: the usual future fears, a lack of sufficiency, the schedule for today, a list of what's needed, papers to be written, the laundry sat overnight again— dang!—and the daughter of the lady I visited in hospice this past week.

A dear teacher's words float in: "Breath deep in the body. Fundamental non-harming. Patience. Dignity."

I sit, inviting my darting attention to rest, noticing each fleeting thought-form and concept, and allowing my mind to be swept clear by the next breath. Each sitting is the *only* sitting, I remember. *Here* is where I belong to myself. I can let go of what I imagine others need from me, settle in, and just *be* for these minutes.

This small window of the morning is where I can practice mobilizing gratitude, openness, and love in the face of our human fallibility and dread, inheritances from every corner of time and space. I let the breath sweep in and clear the field again. Details of the pain in the world rise and fall away. I wonder where my son might be today—is he safe? My heart aches, then one more breath arrives, and I disappear into an empty space.

No self, a temporary mercy.

> *When we see things as they are, we are nobody special anymore.*
> *You can't see things as they are when you have a self.*
> *When you keep saying yes and finding a new self, it takes you into*
> *the unknown. We keep finding a new self and don't know*
> *what it will be. It may feel like freedom.*
> —KATHERINE THANAS, *The Truth of This Life*

This is the way in. These simple, quiet sittings are slowly revealing the skillful means I need to practice in order to work through my attachments, let go of my narrow-minded narratives, and show up with elegance. When I bow some days, it's to a younger version of me. The one who's eating so little to stay skinny, the one who's smoking to relax, the one who works way too much. She's so near I can feel her, and finally, I love her. Each time I go through this process of recognition, I can let her go a little more completely and settle into myself as I am, an earnest, enthusiastic elder in training.

In this glimpse of realization, time folds in on itself again, and I see all the aspects of the people I've forced myself to be, realizing that I am *all* of those people—and none of them.

Letting go of who we *thought* we had to be, we can finally stop grasping and connect with who we are *now*—the intimacy we crave takes shape in that moment of connection.

Your glimpses of your own personal, private peace echo throughout time and space, causing ripples of steadiness. This is the foundation of a settled life.

Who was the person you thought you had to be? Is that construct still lingering in the periphery of your consciousness? Any words of wisdom for that human?

Is there grasping happening in your heart or mind currently? Can you name it, and in so doing, let it go partially or fully?

Have you touched in with your own personal peace?

What is the sense of that experience?

EPILOGUE

Infusing your life with respect.
Joining with your life,
With what's being asked of you, with
how you can serve.
Attuning to your world, with full
acceptance.

Practice,
instructive silence,
more creativity, less judgment,
feeling into something bigger and
more giving.

○

The practice of simply showing up, being present for our
lives precisely as we are, is where we'll linger.

Befriending your history; learning to relate to the past and the present with more compassion and ease, and plain, pure, clear being—precisely what the practice is asking of us.

In writing this book, I've shared my process of dropping the persona I'd built from many layers of discomfort. Instead of chasing and celebrating achievements that mean precious little in the end, I'm choosing to be a student forever, to welcome the process of growing older if I'm given the chance.

The world is fearsome, majestic, painful, and delicate. Our acceptance of daily heartbreak reduces to a whisper every accomplishment chased or coveted. So, I'm building strength in body, character, and practice, holding nothing, heading home on purpose.

Are you with me?

MEDITATION INSTRUCTIONS

When you're ready for meditation, create a safe, quiet corner in your space, perhaps with a small candle. Whether you're seated in a chair or on a cushion, sense the support of the ground beneath you.

Once you've arranged your seat, gently sway your upper body from side to side, then lengthen your spine upright, extending the crown of your head to the sky. Feel your back being supportive and your front body soft, open, receptive. Hands can be in cosmic mudra in front of your *hara*, or lower belly, with palms up, your right palm under the left, with thumb tips slightly touching.

Experiment with having your eyes barely open, your gaze cast down about three or four feet in front of you, practicing a quality of panoramic, gentle awareness.

Inhaling deeply into your belly, collect your attention in the center of your being. As you exhale completely, invite your awareness to settle in your body.

As you breathe, notice thoughts, judgments, feelings, and plans arise and recede. Recalling your intention for practice—to alleviate suffering for yourself and all beings—attune to yourself with a quality of freshness again. Allowing your breath to sweep your mind, bringing your attention back to your breathing, sit for ten or twenty minutes, returning to your breath.

"SONG OF THE JEWEL MIRROR AWARENESS"

The Dharma of thusness

Is intimately conveyed by Buddha Ancestors.

Now you have it.

Keep it well.

Filling a silver bowl with snow,

Hiding a heron in the moonlight.

They are similar though not the same.

Side by side you can see the differences.

The meaning is not in the words,

Yet one pivotal instant can reveal it.

Move and you are trapped;

Miss and you fall into confusion and doubt.

Turning away and touching are both wrong,

For it is like a massive fire.

To depict it with complex words

Is to defile it. In the darkest night,

It is perfectly clear.

In the brilliance of dawn,

It remains hidden.

It acts as a guide for beings.

Its use removes all suffering.

Although it is not created,

It is not beyond words.

It is like facing a jewel mirror;

Form and image behold each other.

You are not it;

Yet it is you.

Like a newborn child,

It is endowed with five aspects.

No coming, no going,

No arising, no abiding.

"Baba wawa" is there anything said or not?

In truth, this has no meaning,

For the words are not yet clear.

Like the six lines of the double split hexagram,

The relative and absolute integrate.

Piled up, they make three;

The complete transformation makes five.

It is like the taste of the five-flavored herb,

Like a diamond thunderbolt.

Wondrously embraced within the absolute,

drumming and singing go together.

Penetrating the source and traveling the way;

You cover the territory and embrace the road.

Complications are auspicious;

Do not resist them.

What is natural and inconceivable,

Belongs neither to delusion nor enlightenment.

Causes and conditions at this moment

Shine completely in the silence.

So fine, it enters nowhere,

So vast it exceeds all bounds.

A hairbreadth deviation

And you are out of harmony.

Through the teachings of sudden and gradual,

Different methods have arisen.

Even though you master such teachings,

The truth keeps on escaping.

Sitting still, yet inwardly moving,

Like a tethered colt, a trapped rat.

The Ancestors pitied them,

And offered them the teachings.

According to their delusions,

They called black as white.

When delusions disappear,

The natural mind reveals itself.

If you want to follow the ancient path,

Please observe the Ancients of former times.

Some try to attain the Buddha Way

By gazing at a tree for ten eons

They are like a tiger with tattered ears

Or a hobbled horse.

With low aspirations,

You will see jewel pedestals, fine clothing.

And with a sense of wonder,

You will see black badgers and white bulls.

Yi, with his archer's skill,

Could hit the mark from a hundred paces.

But when arrow points meet head on,

How could it be a matter of skill?

When the wooden man begins to sing,

The stone woman gets up to dance.

This does not come by knowing,

Nor does it involve ideas.

Ministers serve their lords.

Children obey their guardians.

Not obeying is not filial,

Failure to serve is of no help.

Practice invisibly, work intimately,

Be the fool with no voice.

For realizing true continuation,

Is called the host within the host.

GLOSSARY

altar: A location for deep care, gratitude, safety, and remembrance, altars can be found at shrines, temples, places of worship, and homes; typically small tables, platforms, or shelves on which objects of spiritual significance are placed.

emptiness: In Buddhism, the concept of emptiness is a fundamental teaching that describes the nature of reality, the self, and the path to liberation from suffering as empty of intrinsic nature or substance.

G.R.A.C.E.: A mnemonic device developed by Roshi Joan Halifax to help humans cultivate compassion in their interactions with others. It stands for **G**ather attention, **R**ecall intention, **A**ttune to self/other, **C**onsider what will serve, **E**ngage and end. The G.R.A.C.E. model is based on neuroscience, social psychology, ethics, and contemplative perspectives. It can be used in many settings, including medical systems, education, and corrections. Originally developed for clinicians in end-of-life care, G.R.A.C.E. is now used by a broad range of professionals, including therapists, chaplains, social workers, and teachers.

hara: The Japanese word for "belly," the area between the lower sternum and upper pubis and the lower ribcage and anterior iliac crest, it refers to the center of our spiritual being, a person's true self, or the unification of their physical, psychological, and spiritual dimensions.

impermanence: A core teaching of Zen Buddhism positing that conditioned existence is transient, evanescent, and inconstant.

koan: A paradox or riddle on which one meditates, utilized in training Zen Buddhist practitioners to abandon dependence on reason and logic in order to lean toward a more intuitive insight.

NVC: Nonviolent Communication (NVC) is an approach to enhanced communication, understanding, and connection based on the principles of nonviolence and humanistic psychology. It is not an attempt to end disagreements but rather a way that aims to increase empathy and understanding to improve the overall quality of life. It seeks empathic dialogue and understanding among all parties. Nonviolent Communication evolved from concepts used in person-centered therapy and was developed by the clinical psychologist Marshall Rosenberg beginning in the 1960s and 1970s.

Reiki: A healing modality to activate the natural healing processes of the patient's body and restore physical and emotional well-being.

self-stewardship: Cynda Rushton's definition of self-stewardship is the one to which I turn when I practice this. She explains it as embodying a commitment to know oneself, responsibly and mindfully manage one's resources, recognize and compassionately respect one's limitations, and choose actions that are wholesome and life-affirming.

***shikantaza*:** A Japanese term referring to "just sitting." This Zen practice involves being present, aware, and still without trying to change or do anything.

yoga nidra: A yogic relaxation technique involving guided mental imagery while lying in *shavasana*, or corpse pose. Yoga nidra practice can help invite a deep state of relaxation similar to sleep while remaining aware of your surroundings.

zazen: Sitting meditation, also known as just sitting.

Zen: The Japanese pronunciation of a Chinese word *ch'an*, derived from Sanskrit root *dhyana*, meaning "thought," "absorption," or "meditation." Meditation is at the heart of Zen practice.

zendo: A Japanese meditation hall where Zen Buddhists practice zazen. From the Japanese words *zen* (Zen) and *-dō* (shrine), in Zen Buddhist temples, there is usually at least one zendo, along with a *hon-dō* (main hall) for ceremonies. However, any place where people practice Zen can be called a zendo.

NOTES

1. "Song of the Jewel Mirror Awareness" in Upaya Institute and Zen Center's *Practice Period Liturgy Reader*, www.upaya.org/uploads/pdfs/UpayaPracticePeriodLiturgyReader.pdf.

2. Roshi Joan Halifax, "Grandmother's Heart," October 24, 2022, www.upaya.org/2022/10/grandmothers-heart/.

3. Brian Francis, *Between Two Worlds* (Elsipogtog, NB, Canada: Bear Paw New Media Productions, 2020), 77.

4. Anne Truitt, *Yield: The Journal of an Artist* (New Haven, CT: University Press, 2001).

5. Tracee Stanley, "Altar of the Heart" practice, in *Radiant Rest* (Boulder, CO: Shambhala Publications, 2021), 138.

6. Tracee Stanley, "The Householder's Prayer," in *Radiant Rest* (Boulder, CO: Shambhala Publications, 2021), 73.

RESOURCES

Between Two Worlds: Spiritual Writings and Photographs by Brian Francis

Cultivating the Empty Field: The Silent Illumination of Zen Buddhist Master Hongzhi by Taigen Dan Leighton

The Fruitful Darkness: A Journey Through Buddhist Practice and Tribal Wisdom by Joan Halifax

Gardening at the Dragon's Gate: At Work in the Wild and Cultivated World by Wendy Johnson

"Grandmother's Heart" by Roshi Joan Halifax, www.upaya.org/2022/10/grandmothers-heart/

How to Cook Your Life: From the Zen Kitchen to Enlightenment by Kōshō Uchiyama Rōshi

The Little Book of Zen Healing: Japanese Rituals for Beauty, Harmony, and Love by Paula Arai

The Luminous Self: Sacred Yogic Practices and Rituals to Remember Who You Are by Tracee Stanley

Moral Resilience: Transforming Moral Suffering in Healthcare by Cynda Hylton Rushton

Most Intimate: A Zen Approach to Life's Challenges by Pat Enkyo O'Hara

Not Always So: Practicing the True Spirit of Zen by Shunryu Suzuki

Ordinary Wonder: Zen Life and Practice by Charlotte Joko Beck

Painting Peace: Art in a Time of Global Crisis by Kazuaki Tanahashi

Radiant Rest: Yoga Nidra for Deep Relaxation and Awakened Clarity by Tracee Stanley

Seeds for a Boundless Life: Zen Teachings from the Heart by Zenkei Blanche Hartman

Standing at the Edge: Finding Freedom Where Fear and Courage Meet by Joan Halifax

Subtle Sound: The Zen Teachings of Maurine Stuart by Roko Sherry Chayat

Treasury of the True Dharma Eye: Zen Master Dogen's Shobo Genzo by Kazuaki Tanahashi

The Truth of This Life: Zen Teachings on Loving the World as It Is by Katherine Thanas

Untangled: Walking the Eightfold Path to Clarity, Courage, and Compassion by Koshin Paley Ellison

Upaya Zen Center: all courses and practice periods

What We Say Matters: Practicing Nonviolent Communication by Judith Hanson Lasater and Ike K. Lasater

Wholehearted: Slow Down, Help Out, Wake Up by Koshin Paley Ellison

The World Could be Otherwise: Imagination and the Bodhisattva Path by Norman Fischer

Zen Chants: Thirty-Five Essential Texts with Commentary by Kazuaki Tanahashi

ABOUT THE AUTHOR

Mother, mentor, poet, artist, volunteer, best-selling author, and host of the *Practice You* podcast, Elena Brower graduated Cornell University in 1992 and designed textiles and apparel for almost a decade before shifting her focus to yoga, meditation, art, and writing.

She has been teaching asana since 1999 and studying and practicing Zen meditation since 2020. In 2023, she received the Buddhist Precepts from Roshi Joan Halifax at Upaya Zen Center. Now a candidate for Buddhist chaplaincy, Elena offers her time in hospice and penitentiary settings. Her books walk us through stages of practice, life, and listening.

Elena's Perceptive Parenting audio course is a key resource for parents, and her signature course Simplify brings meaning and efficiency to our daily efforts. She's the founder of *The Matter of Menopause*, a free global podcast series.

Her weekly live yoga practices and meditations are featured on Glo, and her spoken-word poetry can be heard on Above & Beyond's Flow State albums, for which she received an RIAA-certified Gold Record for her writing on "Don't Leave."

Elena works to elevate bright futures for girls and women through her support for Girls on Fire Leaders, On The Inside, and Free Food Kitchen.

01 14

J